FACE

FACE

Sherman Alexie

Hanging Loose Press
Brooklyn, New York

Published by Hanging Loose Press, 231 Wyckoff Street, Brooklyn, New York
11217. All Rights Reserved. No part of this book may be reproduced without
the publisher's written permission, except for brief quotations in reviews.

www.hangingloosepress.com

Printed in the United States of America
10 9 8 7 6 5 4 3 2 1

Hanging Loose thanks the Literature Program of the New York State Council
on the Arts for a grant in support of the publication of this book.

Cover art by Bryan Christie Design

Acknowledgments: Some of these poems, often in earlier versions, have appeared
in the following journals and periodicals: *FailBetter.com, Gargoyle, Hanging Loose,
Harvard Review, Kenyon Review, Margie, Poemeleon.org, Poetry Rattle, Poets.org,
Real Change, Sentence, TrueHoop.com,* and *ZYZZYVA.*

Library of Congress Cataloging-in-Publication Data

Alexie, Sherman
  Face / Sherman Alexie
    p. cm.
  ISBN 978-1-931236-70-6 (pbk.) -- ISBN 978-1-931236-71-3
  I. Title.
  PS3551.L35774F33 2009
  811'.54--dc22

                                        2008046580

Produced at The Print Center, Inc. 225 Varick St.,
New York, NY 10014, a non-profit facility for liter-
ary and arts-related publications. (212) 206-8465

Contents

3. Size Matters

4. Ten Thousand Fathers

for my sons
for my father

Part 1

War Stories

Avian Nights

Starlings have invaded our home and filled
Our eaves with their shit-soaked nests. Rats with wings,
They are scavengers we pay to have killed
By the quick exterminator who sings

In Spanish as he pulls three baby birds,
Blind and mewling, from the crawlspace above
Our son's bedroom. Without a word,
The exterminator uses a thumb

And finger to snap the birds' necks—*crack, crack,*
Crack—then drops their bodies to the driveway
Below. For these deaths, I write him a check.
This is his job. He neither loves nor hates

The starlings. They just need to be removed.
Without guilt, the exterminator loads
His truck with dead birds and the tattered ruins
Of nests: twigs, string, newspapers. It is cold

When he drives away and leaves us, mother
And father of a sick son, to witness
The return of the father and mother
Starlings to their shared children, to their nest,

All of it gone, missing, absent, destroyed.
The starlings don't understand synonyms
As they flutter and make this terrible noise:
The *scree-scree-scree* of parental instinct,

Of panic and loss. We had to do this,
We rationalize. They woke up our son
With their strange songs and the beating of wings
Through the long, avian nights. Then, at dawn

The babies screamed to greet the morning light.
What could they've been so excited about?
What is starling joy? When a starling finds
A shiny button, does it dance and shout?

Do starlings celebrate their days of birth?
Do they lust and take each other to bed?
Are they birds of infinite jest, of mirth
And merriness? How do they bury their dead?

We will never know how this winged mother
And father would have buried their children.
Our son almost died at birth. His mother
And I would have buried him in silence

And blankets that smelled like us. These birds
Don't believe in silence. They scream and wail.
They attack the walls. We have never heard
Such pain from any human. Without fail,

The starlings mourn for three nights and three days.
They fly away, only to carry back
Insects like talismans, as if to say
They could bring back the dead with bird magic,

As if their hungry children could cheat death
And suddenly appear with open mouths.
At birth, our son suffocated, his breath
Stolen as he swallowed his own shit. Faith

In God at such times seems like a huge joke.
To save our son, the doctors piped the blood
Out of his heart and lungs, then through his throat,
Via sterile tube, via the smooth cut

Of his carotid, then sent his blood through
The oxygen machine, before they pushed
The red glow back into him. This was new
Technology, and he lived, though he crashed

Twice that first night, and spent the next five weeks
Flat on his back. His mother and I sat
At his bedside eighteen hours a day. *Scree-*
Scree-scree. We cawed and cawed to bring him back.

We attacked the walls of the ICU
With human wings. *Scree-scree-scree.* Grief can take
The form of starlings, of birds who refuse
To leave the dead. How much love, hope, and faith

Do these birds possess? They lift their faces
And scream to the Bird-God while we grow numb.
The starlings are odd, filthy, and graceless,
But if God gave them opposable thumbs,

I'm positive they would open the doors
Of our house and come for us as we sleep.
We killed their children. We started this war.
Tell me: What is the difference between

Birds and us, between their pain and our pain?
We build monuments; they rebuild their nests.
They lay other eggs; we conceive again.
Dumb birds, dumb starlings, dumb women, dumb men.

Volcano

It was May and we rose early to play
Wiffleball. My big brother was the wiz
And lasered crazy curves past us—one, two,
Three—until we saw that black and gray cloud

Rise above the west horizon. Puzzled
But calm at first, and then surprised
By the cloud's growth—its exponential size—
We rubbed and blinked our eyes, and wondered

What kind of storm was advancing on us
And our little rez. Then my sister screamed,
"I think it's the bomb! We're going to die!"
Suddenly terrorized, we ran for home

Where our mother, usually filled with cries
And wails, whispered, Mount St. Helen's
Erupted." Her calm voice was quizzical—
She'd usually panic in the presence

Of even the smallest of disasters—
But as a fucking volcano threatened
To turn us Indian kids into French fries,
She sighed when she should've been praying hard.

Or maybe I'm prone to melodrama.
I mean, yes, the ash did fall on the rez—
Was knee-deep within hours—and it killed
Some plants and shrouded the buildings and trees,

but what I remember most is that it slaughtered the mosquitoes. Before the
explosion, you couldn't leave your house on a summer night without getting
bit and sucked twenty or thirty times. I must have tasted sweeter than most,

because I'd get bloodied so many times I'd come home looking like a smallpox victim. And then I'd be the brown boy turned white from the calamine lotion. But after the explosion, after the ash filled all the ponds and puddles and abandoned coffee cans, and soaked up all the freestanding water, and suffocated all the eggs, the mosquitoes vanished from the reservation. And they didn't come back for years. So when people ask me what I remember about the eruption, I say, "If the mosquitoes have a word for Armageddon then they were singing it that day." I say:

"If the mosquitoes believed in some God
Before Helen's erupted, then they lost
Their faith soon after the ash fell.
Or maybe a new faith was created

From the ash. What if the mosquitoes formed
Choirs and sang about the eruption?
What if they sang about the deadly days
When so many of them wasted away?

What if they sang high-pitched songs about blood
And the memory of blood? What if one
Mosquito rose out of its ashy tomb
And flew into the glorious sunlight?

O, how would your world change if you knew
Mosquitoes believed in resurrection?"

The Father and Son Road Show

The doctor tells me my father's story,
How he'll die if he stops dialysis.
"First confusion, followed by lethargy,
Then toxins shut off the brain." I hate this

Doctor and his certainty, though I wish
I could hate my father and his weakness.
Of course, I'm lying. Most days, I would kiss
This doctor as he tends the sugar-soaked mess

My father has made of his life. I confess
To loving my father, a gentle man
Whose brutal thirsts have left us all bereft,
And so bereft, I'm to give a command

Performance—a road show, a song and dance—
And convince my father to continue
Dialysis, no matter how he's planned
To die or not die. I don't have a clue

How to begin this time, though I've rescued
My endless father endlessly, traveled
Two thousand miles to buy him a shoe
To fit his amputated foot. Unraveled

By the simple act of living, marveled
By the mundane, my father mowed the lawn
Like van Gogh painted and spread free gravel
On the driveway like God created dawn.

God, how often I woke to find him gone,
Fleeing the children he loved and could not feed,
As if leaving made magic, a spell-song
That conjured fruit, milk, bread, fish, egg, and seed.

Come back, come back, I child-cried, *I need*
My father to return. Now, a father
Of two open mouths (and souls) who need me,
I'm a primitive: I hunt and gather;

I build totems and pyramids; I'm fur
And claw; I believe animals can talk;
I know the world is flat; I'm the cur
Raised by wolves; I worship corn, leaf, and stalk;

A child of the sun, I've learned to walk
Upright but still run on all fours; afraid
Of the dark and fire, in love with rock
And fire, I huddle alone in caves

And pray to my ten thousand gods; I pray
To my father's ten thousand gods; I pray
To my sons' twenty thousand gods; and I pray
For protection, courage, and strength to stay

With my father as he chooses the way
This machine will help him live or not live,
As father and father-son separate,
Loose, broken, dissolved by dialysis.

War Stories

I've got an uncle who punched a man's eye
Straight out of his skull. My uncle died[1]
Young, but the one-eyed man turned eighty-five

Last week. I went to his birthday party
Where he, drunk on whiskey and memory,
Pulled out his glass eye and gave it to me.

"Your uncle hit me with his wedding ring,"
He said, "and scooped out my eye. I would sing
An honor song for him,[2] but here's the thing:

I got no voice. So I'll have to say it true.
Before your uncle's punch, I was closed and cruel,
But now I see more with one eye than two.

I had to lose some sense to get some sense.
Ain't that some crazy shit?" It all depends,
I guess, on context. If the audience

Is willing to suspend their disbelief—
If they trust what a half-blind man can see—
Then they'll discover the beauty of grief.[3]

---

[1] He wasn't really my uncle. I lied.
He was my cousin and he's still alive.
But he really did punch out a man's eye.

My cousin says, "There was war on the rez
In those days. It was always self-defense
When any rez boys maimed any white men."[a]

[2] We Indians love to sing songs about death;
We celebrate war's length and depth and breadth;
We sing more about the life that comes next

Than the one we live now. And we proudly
Carry the flag of this brutal country
And never fret about that irony.[b]

[3] I've got a friend who insists that we red
folks invented the blues. "Who loves the dead
and grieves them better than we do," she says,

And I suppose I would have to agree.
Shoot, if you open our dictionary,
You'll find "indigenous" right below "grief."[c]

---

[a] According to State of Washington Law 9A.16.050, homicide is justifiable when committed either:

(1)   In the lawful defense of the slayer, or his or her husband, wife, parent, child, brother, or sister, or of any other person in the presence or company, when there is reasonable ground to apprehend a design on the part of the person slain to commit a felony or to some great personal injury to the slayer or to any such person, and there is imminent danger of such design being accomplished, or

(2)   In the actual resistance of an attempt to commit a felony upon the slayer, in his presence, or upon or in a dwelling, or other place of abode, in which he is.

So, in defending his Indian-ness, was my cousin practicing a form of self-defense? Well, considering that I am terrified of him—and have never actually asked him about the innumerable beatings he's given to white and Indian guys alike—I hesitate to answer in the affirmative. I think that violent men will always find logical and rational and emotional and compelling ways to justify their violence.

[b] At every powwow, whether in the sawdust of a rez arena or on the carpet of a Holiday Inn conference room, we Indians have a war veterans' dance. We honor them; we sing for them. I understand why we do that. I respect their service and sacrifice. But I dream of the day when we also have an honor dance for those Indian men (and women) who refused to go to war. Can you imagine the beauty of that powwow? Can you imagine the emcee taking the microphone and saying, "This is an honor dance for all those Indians who have never picked up a gun." Can you see them, the Indian heroes, circling for peace?

[c] Of course, my friend, a musician, happens to belong to one of those tribes who think they created everything. Years ago, when traveling with white Hollywood producers in upstate New York, I told them, "Be careful with these Six Nations Indians—these Mohawks and Senecas and the others— because they tend to brag. We call them the Navajos of the North because they're so stuck on themselves." Sure enough, five minutes after we sat to meet with an Onondaga man, he looked upward and said, "It was my people who invented the sky."

In the Matter of Human v. Bee

"If the bees die, man dies within four years."
—a quote attributed to Albert Einstein, but which was
likely created by an anonymous source for political reasons.

1. *For the prosecution:*

The bees are gone.
Who gives a shit?

Other insects

And animals
Can pollinate

All the flora.

We will survive
Because humans are

Adaptable.

The bees are gone.
It's a problem,

But one we'll solve

With good science
And ambition.

Certain bees

Have disappeared,
But the other

More solitary

Breeds of bee
Are still alive

And pollinating

Like porno stars.
Who needs the bees

That are too weak?

Perhaps Darwin
Should be quoted

To prove our point.

The bees are gone,
But won't stronger

Pollinators

Grow in number
And amorous

Intensity?

If you believe
In a good God,

As anyone should,

Then you must know
That God will

Create more bees,

Or replace them
With something else

Equally good,

Because God is
Infallible.

2. *For the defense:*

The bees are gone.
No one knows why,

Not even God.

Some blame cell phones.
Some blame disease.

A few blame God.

The bees are gone.
No one knows why.

If they stay gone

All flora goes
Without pollen

And will perish,

Starved and godless,
Within four years.

The animals

Will soon follow
Flora to dust.

And then we die.

Nothing can stay
Because the bees

Are little gods

Who gave us grace
Bloom by bloom.

The bees are gone.

I sing this song
To bring them back,

Or say goodbye,

Or to worship
The empty sky.

3. *For the beekeepers:*

The bees are gone.
We need new bees

Or we are fucked.

Inappropriate

F. Scott Fitzgerald wrote *The Great Gatsby* in the basement bar
Of the Seelbach Hotel. A few years later, he traveled
First class to Hollywood and let them mutilate his soul.
The great Scott died drunk, penniless, writing-blocked, and alone.

Only after his death did Fitzgerald become a star,
As English Literature professors sought to unravel
The Great Gatsby's tapestries. The slim novel has sold
One hundred million copies since Fitzgerald turned to bone

and is widely regarded as The Great American Novel. I love the book, but I
didn't know that Fitzgerald wrote it at the Seelbach until the night I checked
into my room in Louisville, Kentucky, and read it in *The Luxury Hotel Guide to
Famous Alcoholic Writers*. I was at the Seelbach to give a keynote speech for an
American Literature conference. I spend a lot of time in hotel rooms preparing
to give keynote speeches. It's my job. My speech was scheduled for eight the
next morning—at the *Breakfast Club for Adjunct Professors*—so I went to bed
early, around eleven, but

At three or four in the morning, I heard Fitzgerald's ghost
Drunkenly stumble and mumble down the sixth-floor hallway.
"First you take a drink," the ghost said. "Then the drink takes a drink,
Then the drink takes you." I heard Scott's cocktail glass clink

Against his wedding ring. I heard him toss his tweed raincoat
To the floor. Then he knocked on my door. I said, "Go away,
You bitter fuck." Goddamn, I hate the sweet and sour stink
Of alcoholics. I hate how those damp bastards can shrink

Like mice—no, like rats—and squeeze through the smallest holes
In our walls. "Go away," I said to Scott. "Go back to your grave."
But the ghost slipped under my door, smiled, threw me a wink,
And shambled into my bathroom and threw up in the sink

a disgusting and hilarious act that made me wonder if this ghost was actually my father's ghost hiding behind a mask that made him look like F. Scott Fitzgerald. Can ghosts be that convoluted? I would guess that the haunter is only as complicated as the haunted. And things did become more complicated when Fitzgerald's ghost squeezed some of my toothpaste onto his pointer, and finger-brushed the vomit taste and smell out of his mouth, and staggered back into the living room and sat beside me on the bed. I wondered if Fitzgerald's ghost was going to make a pass at me. I searched my literary memory for any reference to Fitzgeraldian homosexuality. Well, I think it's safe to assume that Nick Carraway, the narrator of *The Great Gatsby*, enjoyed a Platonic and homoerotic crush on Jay Gatsby, so perhaps Fitzgerald had enjoyed a few homoerotic crushes of his own. Maybe Fitzgerald and/or his ghost had a homoerotic crush on me. Wow, I was flattered that the great writer had risen from the grave to rattle his chains in my bed. Or maybe he was just drunk. I remembered a Fitzgerald quote: "Often people display a curious respect for a man drunk, rather like the respect of simple races for the insane." Was I that simple? Was I in awe? Shouldn't I have chased that drunken ghost out of my room or perhaps run screaming in terror down the hallway and into the elevator? Or wait, perhaps one should use the stairs in the event of a haunting. In any case, I neither booted Fitzgerald nor made my own escape. Instead, I wondered how a man is supposed to make love to a man, and I doubly wondered how a man is supposed to make love to a ghost, and then I laughed and awoke

From my Gatsbian dream. "How strange! How lovely! How funny!"
I thought, but soon recalled Fitzgerald's literary advice to "Cut out
All those exclamation points. An exclamation point
Is like laughing at your own joke." Well, fuck that noise!

I am a funny writer! I get paid tons of money
For my jokes! But more than that, I write gorgeous poems about
Chocolate cream pies in the eyes! And wicked kicks to the groin!
I write villanelles that celebrate the counterfeit coins

Nailed to wooden floors! And the fake wasps trapped in honey
Cubes! I once gave a stuffed parrot and eye patch to my gout-
Stricken brother—a limping Captain Kidd—and he enjoyed
The prank so much that his funny bone fell out of joint!

O, his humerus was so humorous! It was punny!
Ah, I wrote a poem about the joy of laughing out loud
While having sex! There's no need to be serious or coy
When one is engaged in that dampest and deepest of joys,

in that most revealing (and concealing) of acts! God, I love to fuck just as much as I love to write poems! Hooray! Hooray! Hooray! Hooray! And I hope my readers are celebrating my hilarity (and pornography), because I also need to tell you something sad and serious. After I woke from my dream about Gatsby's ghost, I sat at my hotel room desk, and I wrote most of the poem you are now reading. And after falling back asleep for a few hours, and being startled into the world by an alarm clock playing Donna Summer's "Bad Girls," I ate room service breakfast—a subject that deserves one thousand heroic couplets—and walked downstairs to give my keynote speech. As usual, I improvised my talk, because that feels more genuine, more relevant to the moment, and more tribally influenced. When I improvise, I feel like I'm standing around a campfire. Which campfire? Any and all of them! So, yes, I told my story about Gatsby and his ghost to the gathered professors of American Literature. I told dick jokes! I told vagina jokes! I insulted Democrats, Republicans, vegetarians, vegans, Indians, and white people! I made fun of my enormous skull, my fat stomach, and my bowlegs! Over and over, I said, "I have so many weaknesses! I am fragile and finite!" I told them that Jay Gatsby—James Gatz—was the first Native American, even if he was actually a German Jew from North Dakota. Yes, Fitzgerald had written the first Native American novel, and in creating a character who believed in the "green light, the orgiastic future that year by year recedes...", Fitzgerald had given me the vocabulary to describe my own Native American identity. Oh, yes, I am the genocided Indian who is also the dream-filled refugee! Oh, yes, I am indigenous to the land but an immigrant into the culture! I am the ironic indigenous immigrant! Yes, I told the room filled with the tenured, soon-to-be-tenured, desperate-to-be tenured, and never-to-be tenured

That, damn, I was full of various kinds of shit and gas,
But that I was desperately trying to convey hope
In our futures, even as I knew that we were "boats
Against the current, borne back ceaselessly into the past,"

and you better believe I improvised and used that final and powerful sentence of *The Great Gatsby* as my own final sentence. Hell, I didn't consciously know that I was going to use it. As I rattled my way to the end of my speech, Fitzgerald's tragic wisdom just spilled out of my mouth. I realized that Indians are now and will always be walking backwards. We will always be contrary. In my mind's HDTV, I saw two million Indians walking together, with their big faces pointed toward the past and their flat asses pointed toward the future, and I laughed. It was sadly humorous! Or humorously sad! And what is humor anyway? Victor Borge said, "Humor is something that thrives between man's aspirations and his limitations." Mel Brooks said, "Humor is just another defense against the universe." Golda Meir said, "Those who don't know how to weep with their whole heart don't know how to laugh, either." Jesus, I gave my heart and soul—and all of the humor in my bones—to that keynote

And, yes, once again, I was paid a shitload of money,
But I tried to create passionate and hilarious art,
So all I could do was weep when I read the comment card
That fatally declared that "All Alexie was, was funny."

Well, that comma between the "was" and "was" was comedy,
But it also conveyed an insult that I can't ignore.
It implied that I'm mediocre—that I'm a laugh whore.
The bastard declared that "All Alexie was, was funny,"

As if delivering a punch line was somehow easy.
Jesus, that comment card made me feel naked and raw,
And illuminated all of my open wounds and scars.
The asshole declared that "All Alexie was, was funny,"

And I drowned in a tsunami of insecurity.
I wanted to go find that pretentious professor and choke
Him into unconsciousness with a book of dirty jokes.
The fucker declared that "All Alexie was, was funny,"

And I turned that little note into a tragedy.
But, no, that won't make me quit. I'll still resist conventions;
Yes, I will disprove the professorial contention
That a serious man is not supposed to be funny.

Vilify[1]

I've never been to Mount Rushmore. It's just too silly. Even now, as I write this,
   I'm thinking
About the T-shirt that has four presidential faces on the front and four bare asses
   on the back. [2]
Who's on that damn T-shirt anyway? Is it both Roosevelts, Jefferson, and Lincoln?

Don't get me wrong. I love my country.[3] But epic sculpture just leaves me blinking
With dry-eyed boredom (and don't get me started on blown glass art.[4] I really
   hate that crap).
I've never been to Mount Rushmore. It's just too silly. Even now, as I write this,
   I'm thinking

That I'd much rather commemorate other presidents. Let's honor JFK's whoring
   and drinking[5]
Or the thirteen duels Andrew Jackson fought to defend his wife's honor.[6] Why
   don't we sculpt that?
Who's on that damn Rushmore anyway? Is it McKinley, Arthur,[7] Garfield,
   and Lincoln?

And, yes, I know there's a rival sculpture of Crazy Horse, but the sight of that
   one is ball-shrinking
Because Crazy Horse never allowed his image to be captured, so which sculptor
   do you think he'd now attack?[8]
I've never been to Mount Rushmore. It's just too silly. Even now, as I write this
   I'm thinking

About George W's wartime lies, Clinton's cigars,[9] and Nixon's microphones, and
   I'm cringing
Because I know every president, no matter how great on the surface, owned a
   heart chewed by rats.[10]
Who's on that damn Rushmore anyway? Is it Buchanan,[11] both Adamses,
and Mr. Lincoln?

Answer me this: After the slaughterhouse goes out of business,[12] how long
    will it go on stinking
Of red death and white desire? Should we just cover the
    presidents' faces with gas masks?
Who cares? I've never been to Rushmore.[13] It's too silly. Even now, as I write
    this, I'm thinking:
"Who's on that damn mountain anyway? Is it Jefferson, Washington,
    Reagan,[14] and Lincoln?"

---

[1] This poem is a villanelle. Many contemporary poets believe the form to be an ancient one (which is yet another example of experts talking out of their asses) but, according to Amanda French (whom Google dubs an "expert in Digital Humanities"), the modern villanelle with its two alternating refrain lines took shape only with Jean Passerat's sixteenth-century villanelle, *"J'ai Perdu Ma Tourtourelle* ('I Have Lost My Turtle Dove')." Passerat's poem, as translated into English, is a terrible, sentimental piece of crap ("I have lost my turtledove: / Isn't that her gentle coo? / I will go and find my love."), but the villanelle form itself has been used in classic poems by many great poets, including Dylan Thomas, Theodore Roethke, and Elizabeth Bishop. It would seem that the villanelle is best used to express the painful and powerful repetitions of grief. I have tried to write a grief-filled villanelle that is also funny ("Funny grief" being the best answer to the question: "What is Native American poetry?"), and while I don't think it's a great poem, or maybe not even a good one, I do enjoy the punning title. Yes, a villanelle called "Vilify." I tried to title it "Villanelle-i-fication," but I just couldn't live with that hyphenated monstrosity (and it now occurs to me that "I Have Lost My Turtle Dove," with its awful sentimentality, terminal nostalgia, and goofy worship of nature, would also be an answer to the question: "Tell me, Native American writer, why do you need poetry?").

[2] At one point in my youth, I owned a Mount Rushmore T-shirt that did indeed feature the presidents' faces on the front and their bare asses on the back. I think it read, "Mount Rushmore from the front! Mount Rushmore from the rear!" I also seem to recall a Tom & Jerry cartoon that featured a chase behind Mount Rushmore that revealed the four presidents wearing only black socks and boxer shorts. Does that mean Tom & Jerry (or Hannah & Barbera, their creators and animators) were political subversives? Or were they just funny?

I don't know. But I do remember that I wore my Mount Rushmore T-shirt to school and was promptly told to go home and change it, as it was "obscene" and "inappropriate for the educational environment." But I don't remember if I wore that T-shirt to my reservation's all-Indian elementary school or to the conservative all-white farm town high school I attended. Would it have been deemed obscene and inappropriate in both places? In any case, I remember that I went home, took off my Rushmore shirt, and replaced it with one that featured a strange cartoon blob-man with his finger shoved deeply into his nose. The caption read: "Pick a winner!"

[3] Native Americans are notoriously and ironically patriotic. During college, while drinking with a few Nez Perce Indian buddies—all of us loudly and drunkenly ranting and raving about broken treaties—a white guy walked up to us and said, "Man, I hate what our country did to you Indians. I hate being American. I hate the United States. It's evil, man, it's evil." One of the Nez Perce guys, the oldest one, jumped up from the table and slugged the white guy in the face and knocked him out. As we dragged our violent friend out of the bar, he shouted, "Nobody gets to talk shit about my country except me! You hear me! Nobody gets to talk shit about my country except me!"

[4] Yes, I hate blown glass art and I happen to live in the blown glass art capital of the world, Seattle, Washington. Being a part of the Seattle artistic community, I often get invited to galleries that are displaying the latest glass sculptures by some amazing new/old/mid-career glass blower. I never go. Abstract art leaves me feeling stupid and bored. Perhaps it's because I grew up inside a tribal culture, on a reservation where every song and dance had specific ownership, specific meaning, and specific historical context. Moreover, every work of art had use—art as tool: art to heal; art to honor; art to grieve. I think of the Spanish word *carnal*, defined as, "Of the appetites and passions of the body." And I think of Gertrude Stein's line, "Rose is a rose is a rose is a rose." When asked what that line meant, Stein said, "The poet could use the name of the thing and the thing was really there." So when I say drum, the drum is really being pounded in this poem; when I say fancydancer, the fancydancer is really spinning inside this poem; when I say Indian singer, that singer is really wailing inside this poem. But when it comes to abstract art—when it comes to studying an organically shaped giant piece of multi-colored glass—I end up thinking, "That looks like my kidney. Anybody's kidney, really. And frankly, there can be no kidney-shaped art more beautiful—more useful and

closer to our Creator—than the kidney itself. And beyond that, this glass isn't funny. There's no wit here. An organic shape is not inherently artistic. It doesn't change my mind about the world. It only exists to be admired. And, frankly, if I wanted to only be in admiration of an organic form, I'm going to watch beach volleyball. I'm always going to prefer the curve of a woman's hip or a man's shoulder to a piece of glass that has the same curves." I have the opposite problem with giant sculptures like Mount Rushmore. They are so literal. Okay, there are four giant heads up there on the mountain. That makes them important, but without knowing the back story, the history, those four giant heads mean nothing. The art only exists with an introduction, with a biography. Otherwise, one could carve any four giant heads onto a mountain and it would still have the same meaning. And what exactly is the meaning of Mount Rushmore? It screams at us, "These four guys are heroes." That's the only message in the art. But I say, "Fuck that, love them or hate them, those four guys were human beings and were far more complicated—far more gorgeous and grotesque—than some epic sculpture on a mountain." I recently purchased a small sculpture from my friend Adrian Arleo. It's a middle-aged man with a satisfied, weary look on his face. He is thick of thigh and belly. He's wonderful. But if you move closer to him and peer through the strange gaps in his body, you will see that a dog is sitting inside of his torso. Why is that dog there? I don't know. But I don't feel stupid by not knowing. I feel challenged. I want to know why that dog is there. I think the sculpture contains the answer. And I will spend the rest of my life studying it.

[5] While reading a book about Robert F. Kennedy's assassination, I learned that some conspiracy theorists believe that a certain former CIA agent participated in the killing. That former CIA agent was half Apache. That just boggles my mind. One never thinks of Indians being the star participants in epic twentieth century events; we're usually just the extras, the brown folks at the edges of the screen. And who would have ever thought of an Apache being a CIA agent? But then again, considering the Apaches' long and violent history—and their aptitude for camouflage and killing—perhaps it was natural for one of them to become a CIA agent. This got me to thinking about Lee Harvey Oswald, who was either a "patsy" in the assassination of John F. Kennedy or was the lone gunman. Oswald was born in New Orleans—the epicenter of American cross-cultural and cross-racial love and lust—so I'm wondering if Oswald had an Indian grandmother or grandfather. Maybe Oswald's rage was already embedded in his DNA. Maybe the plot to kill JFK began when a Cherokee

woman—too weak to walk—fell down on the Trail of Tears to die. Maybe that woman's grandson—Lee Harvey Oswald's indigenous ancestor—saw her fall and die, and maybe he vowed to someday take revenge on the people who murdered her. Damn, now that's a conspiracy theory.

[6] According to the official White House website, Andrew Jackson was "born in a backwoods settlement in the Carolinas in 1767 [where he] received sporadic education. But in his late teens he read law for about two years, and he became an outstanding young lawyer in Tennessee. Fiercely jealous of his honor, he engaged in brawls, and in a duel killed a man who cast an unjustified slur on his wife Rachel." Don't you just love that adjective, "unjustified"? Can you imagine a criminal defendant using that in a courtroom today? "How do you plead, Mr. Jackson?"

"Not guilty by reason of wife slurring."

"Excuse me?"

"The dude I shot—"

"His name is Charles Dickinson."

"Yes, well, I shot Mr. Dickinson because he slurred my wife."

"Pardon me?"

"Man was slurring—talking shit—about my wife. I can't have that."

"What did he say?"

"Well, first of all, he said I cheated him on a horse race bet. He called me a coward and an equivocator."

"Okay, he insulted you, but what about your wife?"

"He called her a bigamist."

"That is a terrible insult."

"Yes, it is, it's not her fault that her first husband lied when he said he had finalized their divorce."

"Wait, hold on a second. Are you telling me that your wife was already married when she married you?"

"Technically speaking, yes."

"So she was married to two men at the same time?"

"Yes."

"So she was, in fact, a bigamist."

"But, your honor, she was only technically a bigamist."

"So if the deceased had called her a technical bigamist, that would have been an accurate, if unkind, statement and not an unjustified slur?"

"Okay, okay, I get your meaning, but the thing is, Mr. Dickinson then published a statement in the *National Review* and called me a worthless scoundrel and a coward. He twice called me a coward. So I challenged him to a duel."

"I see, Mr. Jackson. Well, I understand that you've been involved in a few previous duels."

"I have."

"How many duels would you estimate that you have fought?"

"Oh, I couldn't guess at such a thing."

"People have said it's somewhere between five and one hundred duels."

"I couldn't argue with that. In fact, if you're forcing me to hazard a number, I'd say the number of duels I've fought is somewhere in between five and one hundred."

"So, in essence, it would be accurate to say that you enjoy shooting at people?"

"I feel it's my duty to challenge people who have besmirched my honor or the honor of my family or the honor of my friends or the honor of my country."

"I see. Well, eyewitnesses to your duel with Mr. Dickinson testify that, after he shot you in the chest, your pistol misfired. Now, according to dueling etiquette, that meant the duel was over. And yet, as eyewitnesses testify, you violated etiquette, reloaded your weapon, and shot and killed Mr. Dickinson. How do you respond to those charges?

"I would say that people see what they need to see."

"A dozen eyewitnesses have testified against you, Mr. Jackson. A dozen eyewitnesses dispute your version of events. It's twelve against one. What do you have to say to that?"

"I'd say that one man with courage makes a majority."

Andrew Jackson was also the architect of the Indian Removal Act of 1830, which gave the president power to negotiate the removal of Indian tribes living east of the Mississippi. Among other thefts, blackmails, and broken treaties, the most tragic result of this legislation was the Trail of Tears, in which 7,000 U.S. troops forced 16,000 Cherokee Indians to march west to new lands. Over 4,000 Indians died of cold, hunger, and disease during the march.

[7] Chester A. Arthur became U.S. president after James Garfield was assassinated in 1881. According to the official White House website, Arthur was a champion

of civil service reform. "In 1883 Congress passed the Pendleton Act, which established a bipartisan Civil Service Commission, forbade levying political assessments against officeholders, and provided for a 'classified system' that made certain Government positions obtainable only through competitive written examinations. The system protected employees against removal for political reasons." That's good stuff. Some folks even call Arthur "The Father of Civil Service." In 1882, Arthur enacted the first general federal immigration law, excluding "paupers, criminals, and lunatics," and under his watch, Congress permanently suspended Chinese immigration. That's not such good stuff. Some folks (well, just me, pretty much) even call Arthur "The Father of Kicking the Shit Out of the Huddled Masses, Most Especially the Chinese Ones."

[8] I once thought of Crazy Horse as an Indigenous Jesus Christ, a Native American Messiah, and an Indian superhero. I now realize that he was far more complicated and interesting than that. For instance, Crazy Horse fell in love with another Indian man's wife. Her name was Black Buffalo Woman, and she was married to a drunken fool named No Water. I guess the dude earned his name by drinking his whiskey straight up, no chaser. Well, anyway, Crazy Horse invited Black Buffalo Woman to go on a, yes, buffalo hunt with him. That was not entirely a sexual euphemism back in those days. People actually went on buffalo hunts. These days, if a young Sioux man asked a young Sioux woman to go on a buffalo hunt, it would have an entirely different meaning. Anyway, after Crazy Horse and Black Buffalo Woman returned from their journey, during which they hunted for buffalo and "hunted for buffalo," No Water got pissed off and tried to shoot Crazy Horse in the heart.

"You shattered my heart into pieces, Crazy Horse! Now, I shall shatter yours!"

Of course, Crazy Horse was bulletproof. He'd had a vision that no bullet would ever kill him. And the vision came true. No Water's bullet ended up in Crazy Horse's jaw. Yes, Crazy Horse was shot in the face for stealing another man's wife and he survived. In fact, he prospered. Tribal elders ordered that No Water needed to make restitution for shooting Crazy Horse.

"Here you go, Crazy Horse, here are three horses. They're fast. And, oh, yeah, sorry about the whole shooting you in the mouth thing. You maybe want to go get a few drinks and talk things out?"

The elders also sent a woman named Black Shawl to help heal Crazy Horse's wounds. Of course, they fell in love. And Crazy Horse married her. And, oh, yeah, he was already married to Black Buffalo Woman. Yes, Crazy Horse was married to two women at the same time. They were all living together. Crazy Horse was a bigamist.

[9] Doesn't it seem insane that Congress once impeached a president for lying about getting blowjobs in the Oval Office? Oh, wait, let's make a correction. He was impeached for getting blowjobs in the private hallway outside of the Oval Office. I think, even in his amorous state, Clinton wanted to protect the sanctity of that holy room. Or he was just hiding his adulterous ass. As my friend, Greg, the master of the malaprop, used to say, "Well, it's six of one, or it's six of the other." But let's forget about Bill Clinton for a moment. I want to defend Monica Lewinsky. First of all, I think she is very attractive, a little heavy, yes, but so are most of us Americans, and beyond all that, she has amazing eyes. Gorgeous eyes. And she is smarter than hell. She is now a graduate of the London School of Business, damn it. And one doesn't get an internship at the White House without being a talented and dedicated and ambitious person in the first place. And from all the interviews I've seen with her, Lewinsky seems to be a funny, energetic, self-aware, and rueful, if somewhat immature, person. But let's get back to Clinton. I think the real problem here is that he, as U.S. president, the most powerful person on the planet, took advantage of an intern, the weakest person in the White House. The power imbalance of that relationship turned it into pornography. John F. Kennedy was apparently just as horny, if not more so, than Clinton. But Kennedy had affairs with women like Marilyn Monroe and the wives of other world leaders, and with the wives and girlfriends of Mafia dons. But Marilyn Monroe! Now, there is some equitable power in that romantic relationship. I'm not suggesting that any president should be having affairs, but if, as president, one were thinking about it, one should arrange a Hollywood fundraiser where one could meet famous and gorgeous actresses. If Clinton had been getting blowjobs from Sharon Stone or Kathleen Turner in the Oval Office, there wouldn't have been an impeachment. Now, I might be accused of misogyny here, but I hope you understand that I'm actually rallying against misogyny. I truly believe that we impeached Clinton not because he was a lying asshole who slept with an intern, but because he was a lying asshole who slept with a chubby intern.

[10] Back in 1977 or '78, at Wellpinit Junior-Senior High School, all of the students gathered in the old gym for a musical performance. A guy named

Ben was giving his farewell concert. He wasn't a good student and it didn't look like he'd be able to graduate, so he was looking forward to his GED. But, in the meantime, he wanted to tell us all how much he loved us. And how much he was going to miss us. So he, with the backing of the Wellpinit High School Choir, launched into a full-throated cover of Michael Jackson's hit song, "Ben."

"Wait," my best friend, Steve, said. "Isn't that song about a rat?"

"Yes, it is," I said. "A killer rat."

"Like a super-smart killer rat that leads lots of other killer rats and massacres a bunch of people, right?"

"Yeah, hundreds of rats and, like, eight or nine dead people. Eaten by rats. Chewed to death."

"So Ben, our fellow tribal member, wants us to remember him as Ben the Genius Mass Murdering Mutant Rat?"

"I guess so."

"Wow."

[11] James Buchanan is generally regarded as the worst president in United States history (though I venture George W. Bush will claim the top spot in the coming years). Why was Buchanan so terrible? Well, according to *U.S. News & World Report*, Buchanan "refused to challenge either the spread of slavery or the growing bloc of states that became the Confederacy." Yep, that would seem like a good reason to rank him so low. But, wait, Sherman, can you tell us which U.S. presidents actually owned slaves? Why, yes, my dear readers, I can:

George Washington
Thomas Jefferson
James Madison
James Monroe
Andrew Jackson
Martin Van Buren
William Henry Harrison
John Tyler
James K. Polk
Zachary Taylor
Andrew Johnson
Ulysses S. Grant

[12] The moral logic of Holocaust deniers just murders me. Their arguments all essentially boil down to this: "Hitler wasn't targeting Jews; and besides, millions and millions of people didn't die. It was more like tens of thousands." The Native American Genocide deniers use similar logic: "There weren't 15 million Indians living here when Columbus landed. There were only a few million. And besides, it was mostly smallpox that wiped them out. Only tens of thousands were killed in military actions."

[13] Honestly, I've never been there. This is not a conceit for the poem. I've truly never had any interest in visiting Mount Rushmore or the Crazy Horse Memorial. Once, while driving in the region, I thought about stopping by, but I didn't. I have no regrets. I've seen Alfred Hitchcock's film, *North by Northwest,* where Cary Grant's climactic battle with the bad guys happens on the faces of Mount Rushmore. It's exciting. But I much prefer the ending where we watch Grant and Eva Marie Saint start to make out in their train car, and then cut to the final shot of the awesomely phallic train penetrating a wonderfully vaginal mountain tunnel. I'm a lover, not a fighter.

[14] An excerpt from *The Handbook to Twenty-First Century Inconsequentially Treasonous American Artists*:

"Mr. Alexie, why did you inaccurately put Ronald Reagan's name on the list of presidents memorialized on Mount Rushmore?"

"I'm sorry, but I don't recall."

Part 2

Tuxedo with Eagle Feathers

Dangerous Astronomy

I wanted to walk outside and praise the stars,
But David, my baby son, coughed and coughed.
His comfort was more important than the stars

So I comforted and kissed him in his dark
Bedroom, but my comfort was not enough.
His mother was more important than the stars

So he cried for her breast and milk. It's hard
For fathers to compete with mothers' love.
In the dark, mothers illuminate like the stars!

Dull and jealous, I was the smallest part
Of the whole. I know this is stupid stuff
But I felt less important than the farthest star

As my wife fed my son in the hungry dark.
How can a father resent his son and his son's love?
Was my comfort more important than the stars?

A selfish father, I wanted to pull apart
My comfortable wife and son. Forgive me, Rough
God, because I walked outside and praised the stars,
And thought I was more important than the stars.

Wheat

1.

Three boys climb
The wheat silo;

Two of us
Wait below.

Rung by rung,
The climbers rise

Toward the top.
We strain our eyes

To see, but our
Friends disappear.

We wait and wonder,
But then I hear

The oddest sound,
A soft whistle,

And then I know:
One of them is pissing

From the top.
I run, hoping

To escape, but
Troy, with open

Mouth, stares up
And gets a face

Full of yellow.
Soaked, enraged,

He curses
The humid sky

But I remain
Amused and dry.

2.

Drunk and horny,
My girl and I exit
A high school party
To have sex in

The wheat. It's noon.
I see my girl nude
In the daylight
For the first time,

And I am pleased
To see that her skin—
Her breasts and belly—
Are just as golden

As the summer wheat.
Later my girl and I grew
Apart, but I knew
Her once as she knew me,

Young and tall and uncruel,
And yes, so bountiful.

3.

We weren't vandals,

But we didn't stop
When the local cops

Flashed their lights
Into our teenage eyes.

Panicked, the three
Of us dashed into the wheat.

Suddenly unbored,
The cops were more

Than happy to chase us

Through the small town dark.
Doug and Karl were smart;

They ran around the fence,
But I, being slow and dense,

Sprinted into the barbed wire.
Ah, shit! My chest was on fire!

And I thudded to the dirt.
Bloody but mostly unhurt,

I remained hidden, uncaptured,
And heard the cop's laughter

As they carried away my friends.

Concealed
In that wheat field,

I waited until the cops were gone,
Then ran and made it home by dawn.

4.

Here is a photograph
Of my neighbor's wheat field.

It's just one of my backyards.
As a child, I was surrounded

By wheat fields. Isolated,
I often felt small and rhymeless,

But I was free to roam,
With all of my neighbors' blessing,

In any of their fields.
In this way, step by step, row by row,

I learned how to escape.

Face

Let me sing an honor song for James Bailey,
A pro hoopster who is mostly forgotten,
But who was still playing pro ball in '83
When he, six-ten and clad in white cotton

And new hightops, rose and blocked my shot
Off the court and down the pavement walkway,
Bouncing, bouncing, bouncing, and rolling on a hot
August day until it splashed into Green Lake,

Maybe seventy-five yards away from the court.
That spectacular play shut down the game.
After that humiliation, who can keep score?
One guy asked me, "What's your name? What's your name?"

Because he wanted to get all the details
"Correct." Two other brothers just ran away
And never returned. I suppose I failed
In some basketball sense, by thinking my lame

Spin move running jumper could ever succeed
Against a player like Bailey. But I had game
In those days. Skinny and mean, I could compete
On any court. Or so I thought. How strange

To know, now that I'm old and broken, how young
And foolish I used to be. James Bailey
Was only a decent pro, but I was a runt
In his presence. I'm still a serf, puny

And contrite: "Mr. Bailey, I'm so sorry
I tried to sneak that bullshit into your house.
But, damn, that block of yours was so pretty,
Epic, and canonized by the adoring crowd,

That my embarrassment felt like a blessing,
Like a parable teaching me this lesson:
When we hoopsters look into our interior,
We learn we can be gorgeous and yet inferior."

The Blood Sonnets

1.

When my father left me (and my mother
And siblings), to binge-drink for days and weeks,
I always wept myself into nosebleeds.
And sure, you might think this is another

Poem about a wounded father and son,
But honestly, the only blood was mine,
And it flowed from absence, not from a punch
Or kick. My father, drunk or not, was kind

And passive, and never lifted a fist
To strike. Drunk daddy only hit the road,
And I'd become the rez Hamlet who missed
His father so much that he bled red ghosts.

Years later, in Seattle, my nose bled
When my mom called and said, "Your father is dead."

2.

Ellen, amused, out of breath, informs me
That women know how to turn their bodies
And secretly reach into their dark pants
To check for blood. It's a menstrual Eve-dance,

Earthy and erotic. My wife tells me
That every woman owns a blood story:
The first-date flood or short white skirt earthquake.
Ellen was teaching art once when her dam broke.

Unprepared, wearing bloody jeans, she rode
Her bike home, bathed, and changed. Ellen knows how
To laugh hard, so I laugh, separated
By my gender, but also created

By my mother's blood, so I am, by birth,
A part of all women's blood and mirth.

3.

In the crawlspace, gray feathers in the dirt
Equal dead bird. But no: When I lean close,
I see those feathers are really the fur
Of a dead mother rat. If rats have ghosts

Then I shall be haunted by the small bones
Of the rats who died in their mother's womb,
And the one who was birthed and died alone
In the crawlspace dark. The blood in this tomb

Dried and mixed with the dirt weeks or months back,
But I feel bloody when I shovel
The rat corpses into a plastic sack,
And bury them beneath mud and gravel.

Why do I mourn these rats? Why do I care?
Because even the vermin need our prayers.

4.

Farm town virgins, my first love and I parked
Behind the Spring Creek Grange. The wheat
Fields were snowfields in the December dark,
And I dumbly pushed until her yields

Became acceptance became damp embrace.
Too stupid and quick for condoms, I came
And knew that my sperm was racing toward her egg.
She pushed me away with her hands and legs,

Basketball-muscled, then climbed out the door,
And jumped up and down in the muddy snow
In a Chaplinesque attempt to abort
What we had not conceived. I drove her home,

And we watched *LA Law* with her parents,
Who ignored the bloodstains on her gray pants.

5.

With six shovels, my six cousins bury
My father's coffin in gravel and mud,
Then hug my grief-smacked mother (now married
To dirt) and leave her coat covered with blood

From their blistered hands. This is grief, obscene
And malodorous, sticky to the touch.
This is grief, the city where blowflies feast
And lay eggs. This is grief, one shovel punch

To my teeth, one punch to my mother's neck,
One punch each to my brothers' sparrow chests,
The fifth and sixth to snap my sisters' backs.
Grief, you killer, riddler, giver of tests,

If we lie with our father in the mud,
Will you make us a gift out of his blood?

The Sum of His Parts

Driving home, I ran over a bull snake
And tore it into three pieces.

I didn't mean to kill the thing.
I'd thought it was the thin shadow

Of a telephone pole stretched across the road.
I realized it was a snake

Only after I'd run it over.
Thump, thump:

That's the percussion
Of car tires and snake.

After I ran over it, I stopped,
Left the car idling,

And walked back
To the three pieces of snake.

In death-shock, the head and tail
Thrashed separately

Against the pavement
That had been its warm rock.

The middle piece, strange
And disconnected, did not move.

I said a prayer
To the Snake God,

And wondered if such a God exists.
That's theology.

If the Snake God does exist,
Then it is likely the same

As every other God:
Unreachable.

I didn't want the snake's body to be insulted
By other cars and their drivers,

So I dragged the tail off the road to the west
And the head off the road to the east,

But could not touch the middle piece
Because it was flattened and gory.

Satisfied that I'd shown the snake
Enough respect, I drove away.

But two miles up the road, I turned
Around and traveled back to the snake.

I don't know if there is a Snake Heaven,
But I didn't want the snake to suffer

because of my doubts.
If the snake's three pieces arrived

separately in Heaven,
Would any of them be able to find the others?

I dragged the tail and middle
Across the road and laid them beside the head

Because snake + snake + snake = snake.

Wrist

In *The Age of Innocence*, Newland Archer
and Countess Ellen Olenska, cousins
by marriage, ride in a covered carriage.

I want to write "adulterous carriage,"
But that seems pretentious and clunky to the ear.

However, in looking up the alternate definitions of carriage, I discover that a
carriage can also be:

1. A wheeled support for a cannon
2. The manner of carrying one's body and head
3. An inclined beam that supports the steps of a stair
4. The act of transportation
5. The price of transportation
6. Administration or management

Which means that "adulterous carriage," in the context of this poem, could mean:

1. Adultery is a weapon; or rather, it is the means by which weapons
   are used
2. Adulterers carry their bodies and heads in an identifiable manner:
   the guilt-slump, the prideful spine, the dangerous head tilt
3. Adultery is a small component of a larger system; or in medical
   terms, adultery is a symptom of the disease called troubled marriage
4. Adultery is a journey, though that is a precious and nauseating conceit
5. Adultery has a price, which is obvious, of course, but no less
   painful to realize
6. Adulterers must be clever in order to avoid detection; or, more
   humorously, adulterers are as common and detail-addicted as
   office managers; but then I think how office managers are so
   restrained that any misplaced stapler, memo, or coffee maker
   becomes an illicit object; so yes, I think that adulterers find their
   pleasure in carefully measured cups

And so, with those multiple meanings in mind, and because poems are supposed to have multiple meanings, I rewrite the first three lines of this poem:

In *The Age of Innocence*, Newland Archer
and Countess Ellen Olenska, cousins
by marriage, ride in an adulterous carriage.

Upon rereading, I discover those three lines remain pretentious and clunky to the ear, and are not redeemed by:

1. The exhausted marriage-carriage full rhyme
2. The half-assed rhyme of Countess and adulterous
3. The concussive alliteration of carriage, cousins, Olenska, and Countess
4. The barrage of reptilian sibilants, including innocence, Countess, cousins, Olenska, and adulterous.

My lame poetry suffers when compared to Edith Wharton's description of the adulterous Archer and Olenska:

"Her hand remained in his, and as the carriage lurched across the gangplank onto the ferry he bent over, unbuttoned her tight brown glove, and kissed her palm as if he had kissed a relic."

Jesus, that's a beautiful sentence, enit? And tragic, too. Because that sentence describes the full extent of Archer and Olenska's doomed affair:

He kisses her palm.

Can a palm-kiss be considered adultery? I suppose it depends on the intensity of the kiss and, well, the intensity of the palm. And while Wharton's description of the palm-kiss is elegant, it does lack a certain intensity.

No, it lacks a certain fission.

If adultery can be considered proper, then Wharton has written a display of very proper marital sin.

In the film adaptation of Wharton's novel, as written by Jay Cocks and directed by Martin Scorsese, Daniel Day-Lewis plays Newland Archer and Michelle Pfeiffer plays Countess Olenska.

During the adulterous carriage scene, when Lewis unbuttons Pfeiffer's glove and kisses her palm (and wrist), it doesn't seem that Newland is kissing a relic. No, I imagine that Lewis, using sense memory, is instead kissing lips, breasts, stomachs, vaginas, lower backs, buttocks, inner thighs, knees, feet. And I imagine that Pfeiffer, using her sense memory, feels those lips on every part of her body.

In short, the scene is hot.

Now, I'm not suggesting that Scorsese's movie is better than Wharton's book. Not at all. But I am absolutely positive that the filmed version of the adulterous carriage scene is not only much better than the novel version, but might also be one of the most erotic moments in cinematic history.

All of which reminds me of a woman who once took my hand, brought it to her mouth, and kissed my wrist.

O,

Lord, that was the only time she kissed me.

The Seven Deadly Sins of Marriage

Envy

How odd to be jealous of one's lover's
Long ago lovers, when one should thank them
For their various failures. And strengths.
And odder, this desire to rank them

As she must rank them, but will never say.
Where is the handsome Christian? Or the one
Who said he wasn't married? Or the short
British man whose parents were far more fun?

And what about the existentialist
Who kissed so well she swooned in the street,
But was far too rational to feel joy?
I celebrate the men who preceded me—

Just as the bank celebrates each debtor—
Because they make me look so much better.

Pride

A female fan, upon meeting my wife,
Said, "Oh, wow, you must have a wonderful life
Since you have such a wonderful writer
For a husband. That book, *The Fistfighter*,

Is so charming. Your husband must be charming, too."
And my wife thought, *What a literate fool!*
Only a poet's spouse fully learns the truth:
We writers are the worst kind of cruel,

Because we worship our own stories and poems,
And what human can compete with metaphors?
Writers stand still and yet vacate our homes
Inside our fantasies. We are word-whores,

With libidos and egos of balsa wood.
We'd have sex with our books, if only we could.

Gluttony

If I were single, would I be thinner?
Do I overeat because I don't compete
With the flat-bellied bachelors? Or do we
Thick husbands look and feel thicker

Whenever our wives see a slender man?
Or does it matter? Of course it matters.
I can't stick with any weight loss plan,
·And though my extra twenty won't shatter

Any scales, I despise my love handles,
And often feel ugly and obese.
But my lovely wife always lights the candles,
Disrobes, and climbs the mountain called me,

Because wives can love beyond the body
And make mortal husbands feel holy.

Greed

Every summer, my wife travels to France
To spend a week or two with her good friend.
Of course, my sons and I welcome the chance
To de-evolve and cave it up, and yet,

I sometimes wish that my wife gave me all
Her love and attention. But it's selfish

To want such devotion. There should be walls
Inside any marriage. My wife can wish

For more privacy and solitude
Without me thinking it cold and rude.
She should have friends I rarely meet,
If ever, and I shouldn't let my needs

Become demands, but when I'm most alone,
I often wish my wife was always home.

Sloth

To save time, I put the good pots and pans
In the dishwasher and ruined the damn things.
And, once again, my wife can't understand
How thoughtless I can be. And, again, I sing

The same exhausted song: *I forgot, I forgot.*
When left up to me, the bills go unpaid,
The fruits and vegetables go unbought,
And the master and twin beds go unmade.

Once, when a teacher wondered why our son
Spent so much time lying on the classroom floor,
My wife said, "Because he's seen it so often before."
On a basketball court, I will madly run,

But anywhere else, I will use sedate
Opportunities to pontificate.

Wrath

In the hotel room next to mine, women
Talk and laugh and keep me awake 'til three.
Exhausted and soaked with sweat and venom,
I stare at the walls and think of twenty

Ways to get revenge for their selfish crimes.
At five a.m., as I walk by their door,
I pocket their PLEASE DO NOT DISTURB sign,
And then, from my taxi to the airport,

I ring their room. "Who the hell is this?"
Asks a woman, still drunk and irate.
And I say, "Hey, I just wanted to wish
You a good morning and a great fucking day."

When I tell my wife about my adolescent rage,
She shrugs, rolls her eyes, and turns the page.

Lust

Yes, dear wife, we were younger and slender
(And, damn, I had terrible hair and clothes).
Our marriage was new, exciting, and tender.
Naked in front of me, you still felt exposed,

And I had yet to learn how to touch you
Properly. But now, sweetheart, I've memorized
The curves of your breasts, belly, and thighs,
As you've memorized me, and if we do

Each other less often than we should or need,
Then we can blame time's ground and pound
And not the lack of carnality,
Because, D, I still want to lay you down

Hour by hour, and make you cry for more,
As I cry for you, adoring and adored.

"The Soul Selects Her Own Society"

—Emily Dickinson

On iTunes, I read the "Nothing Selected" icon
As "Nothing Sacred," and I immediately disagree.

"But music is sacred," I say aloud, arguing
With my damn computer. Then I realize my error

And laugh, thinking that entire religions
Have been created because of misprints, mis-

Takes, and misappropriated blame. Take Jesus,
For instance. He never said, "It's better to give

Than to receive." Paul said that Jesus said it,
But a reasonable judge would throw out Paul's testimony

As hearsay, which is cousin to heresy. And I imagine
That plenty of folks would consider me heretical

For questioning the veracity of Paul, but really,
Don't you think that Paul, in a moment

Of self-doubt, when he thought that he was losing
Authority, might have misattributed a quote to Jesus?

If the Son of God was my running buddy,
I'd probably begin every anecdote, psalm, and dirty joke

With "And then Jesus told me…"
It just adds that extra juice, you know?

In my poems, I have given quotes
To my wife for dramatic purposes, and her response

Is always, "I never said that," followed by laughter
Or a sigh, depending on her mood. People believe

What I say; people listen to me. My wife loves me
But she doesn't believe me. The only commandment

I have to deliver is: Writers should not marry their believers.
But that's all tangential. What I want

To say is this: The world was not sacred in its creation.
And it is only sacred in parts. Take, for instance,

A song like PJ Harvey's "To Bring You My Love,"
A blues dirge, which is playing now on my iPod.

It's a gorgeous song, filled with love and lust.
I think it is sacred. But I have to think that

Because I selected it. And if it isn't sacred—
If you download it and think it's only a rock song—

Then I am guilty of bad taste and worse theology
And will become yet another unreliable narrator.

Does the world need one more unreliable narrator?
Well, Jesus told me that faith and doubt are twins.

Do you understand that paradox? Can you live with it?
Can you believe in a messiah who preaches in oxymorons?

The Fight or Flight Response

Years ago, in Spokane, a woman saved
A family of orphaned baby geese.
An amateur ornithologist, she raised
Those birds into adulthood, and then released

Them into the pond at Manito Park,
Where a dozen swans, elegant and white,
Tore the tame geese open and ate their hearts.
Of course, all of this was broadcast live

On the local news. Eyewitnesses wept.
My mother and I shrugged, not at death,
But at those innocent folks who believe
That birds don't murder, rape, and steal.

Like us, swans can be jealous and dangerous,
And, oh, so lovely, sure, and monogamous.

Scarlet

The barista's acne is torrential—
A perfect storm. Whatever potential

She has for beauty has been obscured
By the open wounds that resemble burns.

And yet, as I look closer, I can see
This young woman is quite pretty

Behind her mask. Her eyes are turquoise,
Not some common blue, and her alto voice

Belongs onstage or in the studio.
She makes my coffee and I want to know

Why, in this new age of dermatology,
She suffers this morbid case of acne.

Hasn't she seen the infomercials about creams
And soaps that will make any face clean?

Where doctors and rock stars share laughter
At photos that show the before and after,

And if you want the cure, call this number?
This scarred woman forces me to remember

That my skin was nearly as pocked and razed.
I once counted forty-four zits on my face,

But I was poor and health care was shitty.
I didn't live in a first-world city,

So why does this woman look like this?
She's uninsured and untreated, I guess,

Like so many others, but her poverty
Has brutally tattooed her. I'm sorry,

But there's nothing comforting I can say
To a Hester painted with a different "A."

But, hell, maybe this woman would just scorn
My pretentious allusion to Hawthorne.

She might be an everyday sort of brave,
Someone with no wish or need to be saved,

Examined, and pitied by the likes of me,
A poet who pays, over-tips, and flees.

But then I pause at the door and look back
To see the woman use a fingernail to attack

Her skin. She digs and digs at what wounds her,
Seeking clarity, but nothing will soothe her.

Estranged from the tribe that offers protection,
What happens to the soul that hates its reflection?

Song Son Blue

This is a poem about my goddamn short hair,[1]
And, yes, I know you wonder why you should care.
Ever since I cut mine, people like to stare,
And by people, I mean the handful out there
Who give a shit: those few fans[2] who somehow dare
To ask me about my shorn hair and despair
That I look "so corporate."[3] Are they aware

Of their casual racism? I would swear
At these rude assholes, but it wouldn't be fair[4]
Because my life is public, so I declare
That, after my dear father turned into air,[5]
I cut my hair because of sacred despair.
I'm grieving, you fuckers,[6] so now when you stare,
You'll see the vengeful son[7] returning the glare.

---

[1] My sons had long hair until the age of five.
They can grow it back whenever they choose to.

[2] Without loyal fans, my books would not survive,
But could some readers be a little less rude?

[3] "But, Sherman, with short hair you look kinda white,
And nothing like the rez boy some of us knew."

[4] Do I contradict myself? Yes! And if I like,
I'll contradict God, Jesus, Mary, and you.

[5] This is a bullshit way to say, "My dad died."
He wasn't "dear," either, but he wasn't cruel.

[6] In my back garden, the cannibal plants thrive
By eating the other blooms, stems, leaves, and roots.

[7] I want to be the Hamlet who doesn't whine,
But stands and tells himself, "To do or not to do."

The Gathering Storm

—beginning with a line by Theodore Roethke

All day and all night the wind roared in the trees,
And the thunder woke my sons and my wife.
I held the older, she soothed the baby,
And the blue lightning flashed its thin blue knives.

No, I lied. There was no wind and no trees,
No storm, no thunder, no lightning, no knives,
And my wife and my sons slept easily.
Awake, insomniac, enraged, I lied

About thunder, wind, lightning, knives, and trees,
Because it's easy to lie about death.
A friend from childhood was forced to his knees
By two children who shot him in the head,

And my battered tribe mourns his loss tonight.
But my big brother should tell this story.
He knows about thunder, lightning, and knives.
All day and all night the wind roared in the trees

While my sad brother made plans to carry
Another coffin to another grave.
Arnold, my brother, knows how to bury
His friends. He's buried many. I count names

And faces, and lose track of the number,
But Arnold accounts for all of our lives.
He buried Lightning, he buried Thunder,
And he dug their graves with his thin blue knives.

While my brother mourns, I lie about death.
Death is not a wind roaring in the trees.

Death will never take my sons from their beds.
Death will not force my brother to his knees,

Make him beg, and shoot him twice in the head.
Death won't slash children with its thin blue knife.
Death will pass over us. Death will relent.
Death won't break down the door and come for my wife.

All day and all night my lies roar in the trees.
I thunder and wake my sons and my wife.
She holds the older, she soothes the baby,
And I'm blue lightning flashing his thin blue knives.

Gentrification

Let us remember the wasps
That hibernated in the walls
Of the house next door. Its walls
Bulged with twenty pounds of wasps

And nest, twenty pounds of black
Knots and buzzing fists. We slept
Unaware that the wasps slept
So near us. We slept in black

Comfort, wrapped in our cocoons,
While death's familiars swarmed
Unto themselves, but could have swarmed
Unto us. *Do not trust cocoons.*

That's the lesson of this poem.
Or this. *Luck is beautiful.*
So let us praise our beautiful
White neighbor. Let us write poems

For she who found that wasp nest
While remodeling this wreck.
But let us remember that wreck
Was, for five decades, the nest

For a black man and his father.
Both men were sick and neglected,
So they knew how to neglect.
But then kind death stopped for the father

And cruelly left behind the son,
Whose siblings quickly sold the house
Because it was only a house.
For months, that drunk and displaced son

Appeared on our street like a ghost.
Distraught, he sat in his car and wept
Because nobody else had wept
Enough for his father, whose ghost

Took the form of ten thousand wasps.
That's the lesson of this poem:
Grief is as dangerous and unpredictable
As a twenty-pound nest of wasps.

Or this: *Houses are haunted*
Not by the dead. So let us pray
For the living. Let us pray
For the wasps and sons who haunt us.

A Comic Interlude

1.

David demands that I kill the spider
Crawling across the living room ceiling.
I've killed dozens over the years, feeling
More like a murderer than a fighter,

So this time I try to convince my son
That spiders are hungry heroes who eat tons
Of other bugs—monstrous things with wings
That infest and bite and infect and sting,

But David refuses to understand
The food chain. Or perhaps he wants to assert
The fact that he will never be dessert.
"But, wait," I say, "don't you love Spiderman?"

      "Yes," he says.
      "Well," I say, "if you love Spiderman so much then how can you
hate spiders?"
      After a long silence, he says, "That's a good question, Daddy, I'll
have to think about that."

2.

The next morning, David sees another
Spider on the floor near his brother
Joseph, and both boys panic and run.
"Holy shit!" I yell when I spot this one.

It's the largest spider I've ever seen,
And the eight-legged bastard is hunting me
So I grab a dictionary and crush
The thing into wet pieces, then flush

It away. My boys look at me with awe
Or confusion. They've spotted a flaw
In their father, and though I'd like to walk
Into the next room, my son wants to talk.

> "Dad," David says.
> "Yes," I say.
> "You love Spiderman as much as us, don't you?"
> "Yes."
> "If you love Spiderman so much, then how come you killed that spider?"

> After a long silence, I say, "Because Spiderman is a comic book
character, and that spider was real."

3.

Later that night, I wake from a nightmare
About tiny spiders who infest my hair
And burrow beneath the skin into my brain.
It doesn't hurt, not exactly. The pain

Is more psychological. I can feel
The spiders feeding on my synapses.
They eat my lightning; the bastards steal
My ideas. Jesus, my life will collapse

If I can't tell my stories. How will I pay
The mortgage and keep us fed if I can't sing?
What happens to us if my talent fades?
Or wait, maybe my star has already dimmed.

> "Dad," David says from his makeshift bed on the floor.
> "Yes," I say. "Why are you awake?"
> "I had a nightmare."
> "You have a lot of nightmares, don't you?"
> "Yes," I say.
> After a long silence, my son says, "So do I."

Comedy Is Simply a Funny Way of Being Serious

"Whatever can be forgiven must be
Forgiven." Who said that?[1] Well, it's easy
To look up a quote. The searching is free,
So I type "forgiven," press the return key,
And get eleven million hits.[2] Fuck me!
Is the concept of forgiveness truly
That popular? Or am I just a clumsy[3]

Searcher? I type the whole phrase on the E-
Quote, but that's an insurance site. Fuck me![4]
I'm not a Luddite, so this should be easy.
I search "quote" and "forgiven," find Brainy-
Quote.com,[5] and get five hundred and eighty
Hits, including this by Aesop: "Injuries[6]
May be forgiven, but not by you or me."[7]

---

[1] Of course, you should immediately know
That I invented this quote for this poem.

[2] If you want to fact-check me, then please go
Do your thing, but who the hell fact-checks poems?[a]

[3] A good line or stanza break creates more than a hole—
White space is adjectival inside a poem.

[4] A doubled curse is stronger than one alone,
But should a proper poet curse in a poem?[b]

[5] I don't know which geeks call this site their home,
But I'm lucky that "Brainy" half-rhymed for this poem.

⁶"What a dog I got, his favorite bone
Is in my arm." That's a Dangerfield joke.^c

⁷Of course, you should immediately know
That I invented this quote for this poem.^d

---

^aWilliam Carlos Williams writes, "It is difficult /
To get the news from poems/yet men die miserably
Every day/for lack/of what is found there." Whose fault
Is that? The readers named You or the poets named We?

^bWe know there are irrevocable crimes—
murder, rape, theft, fist to face—but are there words,
or combinations of words, that cross the line,
or worse, grow obscene wings and fly like birds?

^cRodney Dangerfield was a stage name, a lie
That, with each self-loathing punch line, kept growing
Until the Rodney mask completely disguised
The face of a Jewish kid named Jacob Cohen.

^dIt is difficult to forgive the poem
That spends its time in search of the next joke.

In the Mood

In Peter Sellers' most famous role,
He played Inspector Jacques Clouseau,

The bumbling French detective
Whose speech was strangely accented

And shit-your-pants hilarious.
But according to various

Sources, Sellers began to speak
So eccentrically

Only after he'd thrown a tantrum,
Insulted the director, stormed

Off the set, and checked into a Paris hotel,
Where he, while giving the front desk hell,

Heard a bellhop's outrageous accent
And thought, "Clouseau must speak with a French accent

Like this man's." But half of the movie
Had already been shot. "Ah, don't worry,"

said Blake Edwards, the director. "It's so damn funny that the audience won't even notice that Clouseau's accent changes from scene to scene. And if some people do notice the change in accent, then they'll probably think that's even more funny." Ah, Peter Sellers was a strange, cruel, and hilarious man. Did you know Sellers requested that Glenn Miller's "In the Mood" be played at his funeral? Isn't that a funny choice for a death song? But do you know what's even more funny? Sellers hated the song.

He'd been a drummer in a pub band and "In the Mood" was the most common request. How many times must one play a song before one begins to hate it? Does Robert Plant internally weep and wail whenever he hears the first bar of "Stairway to Heaven"? Can you imagine Plant's interior dialogue?

"There's a lady (*fuck her*) who's sure all that glitters is (*fuck gold*) and she's buying a (*fuck stairway*) to (*fuck Heaven*)."

I have a friend, a Jewish singer-songwriter, who has a devastating but ultimately redemptive song about his adventure with a white supremacist taxi driver. The song used to be a staple of his shows, but he stopped playing it years ago.

"I knew it was time to retire the song," he said, "when I was playing it one night and I realized that I was thinking more about returning my rental car than about the subject of the song."

Do you think Glenn Miller ever grew exhausted by "In the Mood"?

Robert Plant is so exhausted by Led Zeppelin that he recently recorded a bluegrass album with Alison Kraus. Yes, Robert Plant, the King of Crotch Rock, is now a bluegrass star.

And speaking of Led Zeppelin, I find it interesting that one of the hardest rock bands of all time also has a song called "In the Mood," which is a rather soft love song, and could very well be the first power ballad. And wouldn't you love to have been at Peter Sellers' funeral when his mourners heard the first bars of Glenn Miller's "In the Mood"?

Hilarious and twisted
After his death, Sellers knew
That his more casual
Friends would likely sing along

But that his lovers and best
Friends would laugh at the old tune.
It was a strange, musical
Tribute, a posthumous bop,

And Sellers' last chance to get
A laugh. Thing is, "In the Mood"
Is truly a wonderful
Classic, and Sellers was wrong

To hate it, though I suspect
He wanted to kill the room
With irony. In control,
From The Average Beyond,

Sellers knew that his request
Of a joyous, upbeat tune,
When played at a funeral,
Would cause more grief than a song

Meant to cause grief. How blessed
Are the humorous and cruel!
But this odd memorial
For Sellers also belongs

To Glenn Miller, trombonist
And big band leader, who grew
Up in Nebraska, started school
In Boulder, didn't stay long,

Then moved to New York instead,
And wrote a string of hit tunes.
Miller was a commercial
Success, but his structured songs

Were often less than respected
By jazz critics. "In the Mood,"
However, is a special
Work of art, one of those songs

That best defines an artist
And his era. This review
Of Miller's life is formal,
I know, and perhaps too long,

but I was trying to write a quiet, murmuring interlude before I called in the
horn section and blasted you with Glenn Miller's obituary. On December 15,
1944, while traveling to perform for soldiers in France, Miller was presumed

dead when his airplane disappeared somewhere over the English Channel. It was one of those wartime mysteries. What happened to Glenn Miller's airplane? Well, it is now believed that British Royal Air Force pilots, short on fuel and struggling to make it back to base, dropped bombs to lighten their load. One or more of those bombs hit Glenn Miller's airplane and sent it spiraling into the water.

When Peter Sellers requested
That Glenn Miller's "In the Mood"
Be played at his funeral,
He knew it would be an odd

Choice, the last comic gesture.
The genius Sellers knew
That Miller's death was unusual—
So bitter, brutal, and wrong—

But it was also slapstick,
Pratfall, spit take, and sick trick.
So bring in the clowns and arsonists
And let them be the church choir.

So stack high the trombones and sheet music
And let that be the funeral pyre.
And let us give praise to the ironic
God who created Friendly Fire.

Heroes

My father was a pilot in WWII.
I don't know how many missions he flew,
But he wanted me to hire a plane
After he died and scatter his remains

Over the farm of our next door neighbor
And mortal enemy. How could I not honor
My father's request? I called in favors,
And a pilot friend and I played bomber,

Flew low, maybe ten feet above the barn,
And exploded my father all over the farm.
His ashes drifted onto the house and plows,
And settled nicely around three dairy cows.

Ah, I was grief-stoned and thrilled.
My father would live on in his enemy's milk

Tuxedo with Eagle Feathers

Six years ago, or maybe it was eight or ten, I went to a powwow at Riverfront Park in Spokane, Washington. I ate fry bread, watched the dancers—especially the beautiful young women shaking their jingles—and listened to my mother and aunts tell dozens of highly sacred dirty jokes. Later that night, after the last dance, as I walked back to my car,

The man who, as a boy, bullied me—
Who screamed, "You ain't no fucking better
Than the rest of us Skins!"—drunkenly
Approached me with an eagle feather

Hand fan and said, "Hey, cousin, can I pawn
This to you?" If I had wanted revenge
Then, I could have bent him like a damn hinge
And left his body to be found at dawn

By some early rising powwow dancer.
But violence is never the answer
(Until it is), so I thought, "What the fuck?"
And gave my enemy twenty bucks.

But don't sing honor songs for my mercy.
I bought those feathers because of pity,

because I realized that I had defeated my childhood bully. I was the rich and famous writer and he was a drunk. No, I need to qualify that. There have been plenty of rich and famous drunk writers; it's my sobriety that separates me from my drunken childhood and my drunken profession. Of course, being sober doesn't prevent me from being a raging, incoherent, vindictive, self-loathing, and needy asshole. But my sobriety does give me sovereignty. Most Indians use "sovereignty" to refer to the collective and tribal desire for political, cultural, and economic independence. But I am using it here to mean "The individual Indian artist's basic right to be an eccentric bastard." I

am using it here to attack Elizabeth Cook-Lynn, the Sioux Indian writer and
scholar, who

Has written, with venomous wit,
That Skins shouldn't write autobiography.
She believes that "tribal sovereignty"
Should be our ethos. But I call bullshit!

My tribe tried to murder me—
And I don't mean that metaphorically.
I've been to dozens of funerals and wakes;
I've poured dirt into one hundred graves;

And if you study what separates me,
The survivor, from the dead and car-wrecked ,
Then you'll learn that my literacy
Saved my ass. It was all those goddamn texts

By all those damn dead white male and female writers
That first taught me how to be a fighter,

so let me slap Cook-Lynn upside her head with the right hand of John Keats
and the left hand of Emily Dickinson. Let me kick her in the shins with the
left toe of Marianne Moore and the right toe of John Donne. I wasn't saved
by the separation of cultures; I was *reborn* inside the collision of cultures. So
fuck Cook-Lynn and her swarm of professorial locusts. But wait, literary pre-
tensions aside, here I am, dry-drunking my way down the page. Instead of
insulting Cook-Lynn's ugly fundamentalism, why don't I celebrate beauty?
Why don't I celebrate Dorothy Grant, the Haida fashion designer and artist?
O, Dorothy Grant, who blends traditional Haida symbol and imagery with
twenty-first century fashion. O, Dorothy Grant, who makes tuxedos with gor-
geous eagle ravens flying up the lapels. O, let me tell you about

A June day in a Target parking lot
Where I waited to meet Ms. Dorothy Grant.
On the phone, we'd agreed it was an odd
Place to try on a formal coat and pants,

But I needed a tux within a week,
And she happened to have a 44
Regular that she thought might fit me.
I had never met Dorothy Grant before

But I recognized her when she drove up
In her hybrid car. She pulled the black tux
Out of her trunk and handed it to me.
Unafraid of some partial nudity,

I pulled on the pants and coat. But, shit, shit,
Dorothy Grant's gorgeous clothes did not fit,

and I howled with pain and shame. "Looks like you've had a little too much
commodity cheese," Dorothy said and laughed. I laughed, too. I am a big-
shouldered man with a belly and thin legs. "I'm just like every other Indian
guy," I said to Dorothy. "I'm built like a chicken. Do you have a tuxedo sized
for a giant human chicken?" "All of my tuxedos are made for Indian guys,"
she said. "So they're all sized for giant human chickens." We laughed. "Well,"
I said. "I can't buy this one but maybe you can make me a custom one in
the future?" "Anytime you want," she said. I was happy to meet her and, as
I stood there in the Target parking lot in Albuquerque, I studied the careful
stitching in Dorothy's garment. Ah, it was hand-sewn! Ah, it was so formally
constructed! "Hey," I said. "Let me hug you goodbye while I'm wearing your
design." And so we hugged. As I changed back into my street clothes, I told
Dorothy that I was going to write a poem about her. "What kind of poem?"
she asked. "A hybrid sonnet sequence," I said. "An indigenous celebration of
colonialism or maybe a colonial celebration of the indigenous. O, Dorothy, it's
going to be a hand-sewn sonnet! You'll be able to count the stitches!" And
so, here it is, but

This sonnet, like my reservation, keeps
Its secrets hidden behind boundaries
That are simple and legal at first read
(Fourteen lines that rhyme, two rivers that meet,

Poem and water joined at one confluence),
But colonialism's influence

Is fluid and solid, measurable
And mad. If I find it pleasurable

To (imperfectly) mimic white masters,
Then what tribal elders have I betrayed?
If I quote Frost from memory faster
Than I recall powwow songs, then what blank

Or free or formal verse should I call mine?
I claim all of it; Hunger is my crime.

Chicken

The sun illuminates only the eye of the man,
But shines into the eye and heart of the child.
—Ralph Waldo Emerson, *Nature*

My wife wanted to give my sons the chance
To see my tribe's powwow with transparent eyes,
And maybe fall in love with the chicken dance,

But I stayed home. They wouldn't hear my crazy rants
About the powwow bullies who made me cry.
My wife wanted to give my sons the chance

To enjoy themselves. "Listen, I just can't
Go with you," I said to my wife, who was unsurprised
By my need to spin a different chicken dance.

"They can hang with their uncles and aunts,"
I said. "And my mother, she'll be so surprised
That my sons have been given the chance

To powwow." And so my wife and sons drove, *sans*
Father, to my rez on a Saturday night
And spent hours watching the chicken dance.

And, yes, I remember pissing my pants
When I saw the reds of my bullies' eyes,
But my wife gave my sons an aboriginal chance.

"Your boys saw joy in their uncles and aunts,"
My wife said, "And the pride in your mother's eyes,
So be thankful I gave your sons this chance
Because they fell in love with the chicken dance."

Grief Calls Us to the Things of This World

The morning air is all awash with angels
—Richard Wilbur, "Love Calls Us to the Things of This World"

The eyes open to a blue telephone
In the bathroom of this five-star hotel.

I wonder whom I should call? A plumber,
Proctologist, urologist, or priest?

Who is blessed among us and most deserves
The first call? I choose my father because

He's astounded by bathroom telephones.
I dial home. My mother answers. "Hey, Ma,"

I say, "Can I talk to Poppa?" She gasps,
And then I remember that my father

Has been dead for nearly a year. "Shit, Mom,"
I say. "I forgot he's dead. I'm sorry—

How did I forget?" "It's okay," she says.
"I made him a cup of instant coffee

This morning and left it on the table—
Like I have for, what, twenty-seven years—

And I didn't realize my mistake
Until this afternoon." My mother laughs

At the angels who wait for us to pause
During the most ordinary of days

And sing our praise to forgetfulness
Before they slap our souls with their cold wings.

Those angels burden and unbalance us.
Those fucking angels ride us piggyback.

Those angels, forever falling, snare us
And haul us, prey and praying, into dust.

Part 3

Size Matters

The Oral Tradition

Years ago, in Eugene, Oregon, a woman introduced me to a small audience with this:

"After fucking my married lover twice, as we dozed in each other's sweat, he suddenly jumped out of bed, and said, 'You have to hear this guy's poems.'

So he runs to his shelf, pulls down this little book of poems called *The Business of Fancydancing*, and starts reading aloud. Reads the whole damn thing, and it's wonderful.

My naked lover, great poems, and the smell of sex lingering. Can you imagine a better day?

And that, ladies and gentlemen, was the first time I ever heard of Sherman Alexie."

I laughed, of course. It was a hilarious
Ode to the poetic and adulterous,

But it's also when I first realized
(And please forgive my naïve surprise)

That poets will give you affection
As they steal the audience's attention.

Of course, I'm no better than the rest.
I turn each reading into a test

Of my humor and masculinity.
It's cheap, but I want strangers to want me

Naked on their shelves if not in their beds.
Who doesn't know that reading is like sex?

Well, after that introduction, I spoke
About my father and my father's ghost,

Like I always do, and though I was bored
With myself, I was still keeping score

And counted the women whose eyes betrayed
Carnal ambition: *Ah, that one would play*

With me, and so would that one and that one.
That blonde in the back would be the most fun.

And yes, you might think this poem is callow,
But there are poets—wise on paper, hollow

In person—who are famous for sleeping
With their groupies. Who doesn't know reading

Is like sex? Who doesn't know that lovely
And lonely women seek the company

Of homely poets? Me, I like to go back
To my hotel room and lustily attack

Myself. I'm the Mayor of Masturbation
City (and yes, for your information,

I know this poem is pleasuring itself),
But, please, I do need your patience and help.

I'm trying to feel my way to the reason
Why this poem exists: Think of a season,

Your favorite one, and allow its weather
To become your weather. This poem gets better

If you let yourself feel summer heat
Or autumn melancholy or winter freeze,

Or even the non-ironic hope of spring,
Because, and now I'm getting to the thing,

I want you to know that the naked guy
Who read my poems aloud eventually died

Of lung cancer. I learned this from his wife,
Who introduced herself to me one night,

Years later, just after I retold this story.
"That was my husband," she said, so weary,

It seemed, of loving adulterous ghosts.
I'd just turned her into an anecdote,

But she was forgiving and somehow amused,
While I felt stupid, silly, and cruel.

She said, "I always knew he'd return to me,
And he did. He left that woman. A week

Later, he coughed up a handful of blood.
One month after that, my husband was gone."

What could I say? "Shit," I said. "Shit, shit."
I'd lost my talent for words, warmth, and wit.

But with a grace so pristine and wicked,
The woman said, "He always looked good naked,

Especially when he was reading in bed."
Who doesn't know poetry is just like sex?

Nudity Clause

They're real. And they're spectacular.
—Teri Hatcher, *Seinfeld*, Episode 59

I have a beautiful friend, an actress
Who appeared in a few films before she retired
To pursue another career. Her last role
Was her biggest (she was third-billed),
And I went to the Hollywood premiere.
The movie was immediately bad, but I endured
And waited for my friend to enter the story,
And when she did, I sat back and gasped
Because she was naked and naked and naked

And naked. Of course, I'd always been aware
Of my friend's extraordinary beauty,
And I'd entertained a fantasy or two
About her, but I'd never pursued her.
I'm married; so is she. Watching my friend,
Naked and twenty feet tall, I felt terrible
Because I was aroused. Was I betraying
My wife, my friend, and her husband
By so publicly lusting? Of course not!

My soul can't be blamed for my body's reflexes.
And yet, I wanted to skip the after-party
Because I didn't want to face my friend.
But I didn't want to disappoint her
Just because of my timidity. So I went to the party
And greeted my friend and her husband.
"Sherman!" she said. "Thank you for coming!
What did you think of the movie?" I wanted
To say, "Horrible flick, wonderful breasts,"

But who says a thing like that aloud (except
In a poem)? Instead I said, "The movie was okay,
But you were great." And she was, better
Than she'd ever been. She was ethereal and tough.
I wanted to ask her why she hadn't warned me
That she'd be so damn naked, but then I realized
That her nudity was necessary and natural
For her part in this period film. Of course
She was naked. Why wouldn't she be naked?

It would have been anachronistic if she were clothed.
And so mollified and satisfied by my logic,
I hugged my friend and predicted great things
For her (if not for the film), and then left
The party (I hate parties) and went back to my hotel.
Once there, I took off my clothes and called my wife.
"I'm naked and horny," I said. My wife laughed
And asked, "What kind of movie did you just see?"
Honey, it was a farce about colonial discovery.

Naked and Damp, with a Towel around My Head, I Noticed Movement on the Basement Carpet

Ants invaded our home, our walls, ceilings, and floors.
I killed the little red bastards by the dozens,
But they would not retreat or surrender. They warred

Like Phil Sheridan and his illiterate corps
Of cavalry grunts. And though it's been a dozen
Years since I left the rez, its walls, ceilings, and floors

Thick as a prison's, I recall how to be poor,
That you must punch your siblings and kick your cousins,
And then share the wormy government food. My war

With the ants was blasphemous. What kind of profane boor
Wants to genocide his sacred little cousins?
Shouldn't I share my home's walls, ceilings, and floors

With any hungry souls? Fuck the ants! I felt poor
Again, like a rez urchin, as if a dozen
Years of peace and joy had been destroyed by the war

With these terrorists. Tell me, what's worth fighting for?
I killed and killed and killed and killed my ant cousins.
I protected my home, my walls, ceilings, and floors,
Because the rich must always make war on the poor.

Mystery Train

I boarded the Amtrak in Portland on my way
To Seattle and searched for an empty seat—
Hopefully an empty row. In Coach Car C,
I saw a seat next to a teen. The train swayed

As I approached him and asked, "Can I sit here?"
He wouldn't look at me. His face was blank.
Asberger's, I thought. "I must warn you I'm weird,"
The kid said. "I'm weird, too," I said and thanked

Him for his kindness. I worried he would talk
Too much, and he did, but he was charming and rude.
He said, "You've got a big head and face, dude."
He said, "I like rap music more than I like rock

Because I like blacks more than whites,
Especially when I play the royal game, chess."
With Asberger's, I knew the kid might obsess
Over certain objects or ideas, like

The boy I know who collects Matchbox cars
And recites the manufacturing history
Of thousands of them. "It's not too far,"
The kid said. "We are on a train journey,

But I take it twice a month, on weekends.
I'm sorry I'm weird. I don't have many friends.
My mother and father love me, but they
Got divorced when I was ten. You could say

They hate each other as much they love me."
He told me his father lived in Portland
And his mother in Seattle. "It's kind of fun
To ride the train," he said. "I like to see

The landscape out the window. Pretty soon,
There will be a yellow truck parked outside
A blue and red house." Of course, he was right.
As we traveled north, the kid always knew

What was coming next. I asked, "What's your name?"
He ignored me and said, "There used to be
A dog that lived in that junkyard. It's a shame,
But I think he's dead now." Then he looked at me,

Made eye contact for the first time, and said,
"In seven years, I have taken this trip
One hundred and nine times. I have only missed
Two trains because I had the flu in my head."

Jesus, the kid had become a nomad
Riding the rails through the ruins of a marriage,
And, at first, I was eager to disparage
His parents, but then I realized that

His folks must love him as obsessively
As he loves them. They put him on the train
Because they need to see him. It was lovely
And strange. I wanted to ask this kid about pain

And what that word meant to him. I guessed
He could teach me a new vocabulary—
I was vain and wanted to be blessed—
But then he asked, "Are you old and married?"

"Yes," I said. "I've been married for ten years."
He nodded his head and looked out the window
At the sunlight flashing between tree rows,
Then whispered, "I have cried a lot of tears."

I was breathless. Stunned. I wanted to take
The kid into my arms, but I knew he'd hate
The contact, so I could only smile
When the kid said, "In a little while,

We are going to see the Mima Mounds."
And there were thousands of those things, six
To eight feet tall, dotting the South Sound.
Created with gravel, rocks, dirt, and sticks,

Those mounds escape explanation. They're not
Indian burial sites. They're not homes
For gophers or insects. They don't contain bones
Or fossils or UFOs. They're just odd

Geologic formations that will keep
Their secrets no matter how hard we try
To reveal them. When our train arrived
In Seattle, the kid walked beside me—

I had quickly become a habit, I guess—
Until he saw his mom, short and pretty,
And pulled her tightly against his chest.
He said something to her, pointed at me,

And she smiled and waved. I walked home,
Chanted the first lines of this poem,
And committed them to memory.
And if a few strangers thought me crazy

For writing poetry, aloud, in public,
Like just another homeless schizophrenic,
Then fuck them for wanting clarity
And fuck them for fearing mystery.

Bird-Organ

A *small barrel-organ used in teaching birds to sing*
—John Ogilvie, *The Comprehensive English
Dictionary,* London, 1865.

Ah, canary, you chronic mimic,
Do you find any joy in the cover song?
Of course, you must. You're an echo addict
Who can't stop himself from singing along

With the bird-organ. It's an odd machine,
Rather arrogant, in fact. What asshole
Believes a wooden box's melody
Is more beautiful and original

Than the canary's indigenous croon?
What kind of blasphemous, hell-bound dickwad
Thinks a man's hands are more clever than God's?
Well, I'm a sinner in love with iTunes

And that lovely manmade box, the iPod.
And if that gets me in trouble with God,

Then may God's lightning fingers choke me dead,
Because I think the Flaming Lips' cover
Of "I Can't Get You Out of My Head"
Is filled with far more fear, lust, and wonder

Than Kylie Minogue's worldwide dance hit.
Okay, now, maybe you don't give a shit,
But my theory (and it's a betrayal
Of my tribe) is that art is colonial,

And the best art is imperialistic.
I know it's wildly masochistic
For an Indian to advance this belief,
But I'm also a Picassoesque thief,

A carnivorous and scavenging bird
Who'll echo, borrow, and steal your words

If given the chance. There is no treaty
I will not bend, bust, ignore, or screw.
But, no, wait, that's not exactly true.
I don't write about sacred ceremonies,

And I rarely speak the names of the dead—
Though I'm going to violate those taboos
Right now in this poem. I suspect you knew
That I break promises with each breath,

But trust me when I tell you this story:
Years ago, a white archeologist
Recorded a tribal ceremony
On my rez. The tape crackles and hisses,

But one can clearly hear my grandmother
Singing. O, her voice comes from some other,

Alien place in her body. That song
Died with my grandmother, or so you'd think,
But whenever I want to hear her sing,
I just press play on my boom box. It's wrong,

I suppose, to worship a duplicate,
But I think, "Screw you, it's decades too late
To save the original." I'll worship
My grandmother's voice and the Flaming Lips,

Live or recorded. I guess, near the end,
I am arguing against nostalgia.

I will not believe "it was better then."
After all, each of us is a replica,

And I think God gave us these music toys
So we can create and hoard glorious noise.

How to Create an Agnostic

Singing with my son, I clapped my hands
Just as lightning struck.

It was dumb luck,
But my son, in awe, thought

That I'd created the electricity.
He asked, "Dad, how'd you do that?"

Before I could answer, thunder shook the house
And set off neighborhood car alarms.

I thought that my son, always in love with me,
Might fall to his knees with adoration.

"Dad," he said. "Can you burn
down that tree outside my window?

The one that looks like a giant owl?"
O, my little disciple, my one-boy choir,

I can't do that because your father,
Your half-assed messiah, is afraid of fire.

Psalm 101

"The thing is," she says, "how come there are so many poems about blood oranges and pomegranates?"

"I don't know," I say.

"Do you even know anybody who's eaten a blood orange or pomegranate?"

"I've got a friend who used to love blood oranges, but she can't eat them now because of the citric acid."

"How about pomegranates?"

"My dad bought them once, on our way to Disneyland, in Redding, California, or somewhere like that. And we all shared a few of them. But, damn, it took forever to eat, picking out those little seeds. I mean, they were good, but you only tasted them for, like, a nanosecond, and then you had to dig for hours to get another one."

"So were they worth all the hard work?"

"No, not really."

"See there, in all those mystical poems about pomegranates, has anybody once mentioned how hard they are to eat? I don't remember ever reading a poem called 'The Difficult Fruit: Maybe Not Worth the Effort'. Do you ever remember reading anything remotely honest like that?"

"No, but pomegranates are filled with antioxidants, aren't they? People love their antioxidants. They're putting it in personal ads: 'Single White Female in search of Single White Male. Must be tall, handsome, and antioxidant.'"

"Listen, I love antioxidants, too, but that's not what I'm talking about."

"What are you talking about?"

"I'm saying that poets always celebrate the difficult, obscure shit. Or the difficult, obscene shit. I mean, poets like blood oranges because they can get all sexual with the moist pink triangular slices, or get all violent with the bloody juice, or get all sexual and violent at the same time."

"That's true. I wish somebody would write a poem about a simple fruit, something like the Granny Smith apple."

"Poets aren't going to use the Granny Smith apple, because the name sounds funny. You can't put the word 'Granny' in a poem. Nobody will take you seriously if you put the word 'Granny' in your poem."

"Use the word 'Granny' and they'll call you a regionalist."

"And once they call you a regionalist, your career is fucked. Because you look up 'regionalist' in the poetry dictionary and you know what it says?"

"What?"

"It says 'Lonely white woman from the suburbs or overeducated brown guy who is the estranged son of migrant farm workers.'"

"You know what? Fuck them. I'm going to write a poem about the Granny Smith apple. I'm going to celebrate that common fruit."

"Thing is, I was just thinking and, in, like, Japan, the Granny Smith is pretty rare. Really expensive, I guess."

"Okay, so maybe my poem won't make any sense in Japan. But I'm not writing it in Japan. Last time I checked, Japanese consumers were not rushing out to buy my poetry. They might be spending hundreds of dollars on Granny Smith apples, but they ain't spending shit on me. So, I say, just in terms of this poem, 'Fuck Japan.'"

"No, no, no, you don't say, 'Fuck Japan.' That could easily be interpreted as being racist. It will bring a subtext to your Granny Smith poem you don't want. What you're really saying is, 'Fuck the exotic.'"

"Okay, now I know you're using 'fuck' in a negative sense there, in a violent and dismissive way, but if you think of it as a sexual act, then 'Fuck the exotic' is kind of cool and lusty. I mean, don't we all, when it comes right down to it, want to 'Fuck the exotic?' Or at least fuck exotically?"

"Yeah, you're right. And all those damn poets are writing those poems about blood oranges and pomegranates because they want to have exotic sex with the exotic."

"Yeah, and I want my poem about Granny Smith apples to have an entirely different meaning. I want my poem to say, "Fuck the fruit that has been on every one of my shopping lists for the last twenty-three years.'"

"And by 'fuck,' you mean—"

"I mean 'sex.'"

"Good, good. But make sure it has other meanings than the whole sex thing, okay?"

"I'll try."

"And can you maybe make it into a little prayer?"

"I always do."

"Okay, good, because people will know you mean it if it sounds something like a psalm."

"Okay, then, here's your psalm."

I come to honor the produce of our prodigious planet.
I think the Granny Smith apple is an underrated fruit.
So why are there so many poems about blood oranges and pomegranates?

Why have those eccentric tropes become the metaphoric standard?
Shouldn't one write about the fruits that one actually consumes?
I come to honor the produce of our prodigious planet,

Because certain poets take the common flora for granted.
I think I can turn the Granny Smith apple into something new,
So why write one more poem about blood oranges and pomegranates?

The Granny Smith apple is more sour and sharp to our palate
Than other apples. The Granny's scent can suppress our lust for food,
So we won't overeat the produce of our prodigious planet.

Before one bites a Granny Smith apple, one must understand its
Magical properties. Or perhaps I'm overselling this news.
After all, the endless poems about blood oranges and pomegranates

Are so ethereal and liquid that I want to damn them,
But the Granny Smith apple is a solid and secular fruit.
While other poets mythologize blood oranges and pomegranates,
I come to honor the ordinary produce of our ordinary planet.

Crow Boom

*...despite all the crow poems that have been written
because men like to see themselves as crows...*
—Lucia Perillo

Crow grabbed a robin
In the rare blue sky,
And crashed the smaller
Bird down to the street

In front of my home.
I watched crow talon-
Crush that robin's bones
And dig out marrow

And shard. Did that crow,
Like human hunters,
Believe it absorbed
The dead robin's soul

By eating its brain?
Do crows fly faster
With each bird they eat?
Imagine a crow

So good at the hunt,
And stuffed with songbirds,
That it breaks the speed
Of sound. I praise crows,

Not because I see
Myself as a crow,
But because they hunt.
I'm not a hunter,

But I need to eat
What my hunters kill.
So I praise hunters
Because I want them

To deliver food
To me. I give thanks
For my food because
All food is holy

And deserves our praise.
I praise the robin
That died for the crow.
I praise animals

Who are killed for me.
I praise every piece
Of these animals
Because every piece

Is holy. I praise
Skin, sweetmeat, and grease.
All grease is holy.
I thank God for grease.

I thank God for root.
I praise vegetable
And grain. I praise fruit
And seed. I praise blood

And brain. I praise
Death because I am
Alive and will die,
If not at the hands

Of another man,
Then by the slow hunt
Of mortality.
Walking dead, I am

Nobody's hunter,
But I will be food,
And hope to be praised
By bacteria,

And honored by flies,
Beetles, wasps, and mites.
I hope that my blood
And flesh fuel the flight

Of crow and robin.
I hope that I stay
Alive in the bones
Of hunter and prey.

I hope that my soul,
Masculine and vain,
Becomes oxygen
Or a good hard rain.

Do these hopes make me
An arrogant man?
If so, then I praise
Male arrogance.

I praise our dark brows
And our crow-black hair.
I praise our cock struts
And avian sneers,

Because I'm in love
With our terrible
And tender world.
I'm in love with men,

Who are lovelier
And more dangerous
Than a simple crow.
But I will be just

And pay for the right
To venerate crow.
I will give my crow
A stipend of one

Fresh robin for each
Time he flies his way
Into my proud poems,
Because men need crows

To remind us how
To be better men,
Stuffed with songs of praise
And quickened by faith.

Small Ceremonies

During the night, a spider built its web
In and around our mailbox. I search
For the thing, hoping it doesn't have a red
Hourglass on its belly, before I reach

Into the box—brushing aside the web,
Breaking the whole into fine sticky threads—
And pull out catalogs, postcards, ads, dead
Letters, bills, sweepstakes, all the evidence

Of an ordinary life. This happens
Every morning for a week. I destroy
What the spider creates. Human sadness
And spider sadness, my joy and its joy

Are alien emotions. The unseen
Spider might be incapable of grief
At this destruction. It might never weep
Or mourn its losses. Does this spider need

To celebrate the daily construction
And reconstruction of its web, its home,
Its killing floor? I only ask these questions
Because I want to confess and atone

For the small sin of valuing my life
More than the life of this nameless spider,
Who rebuilds its damn web for seven nights.
This eight-legged architect, street fighter,

Union worker and guerilla soldier
Will not surrender to me. I admire
This spider, though what I see as boldness
Is likely the dumb instinct to survive

And replicate, to give birth, to mother
Hundreds of children, to construct these webs,
Each one identical to the others,
To repeat, repeat, repeat until death.

On the eighth morning, the spider is gone.
Briefly, I grieve this loss and am surprised,
Briefly, by my grief, before I return,
Return, return to my life, dumb and brief.

A-Gatewards

"To go a-gatewards *was therefore to conduct a guest toward the high-road, the last office of hospitality, necessary for both guidance and protection...."*

        —Jeffrey Kacirk, *Word Museum: The Most Remarkable English Words Ever Forgotten*, citing Joseph Hunter, *The Hallamshire Glossary*, 1829.

In other days, after dark, proper hosts
Stepped into good boots and guided their guests
Through unmapped woods or swamp to the known road—
The public highway—and only then said

Their good nights. In our days, the wilderness
Is less than wild, and thoroughly mapped—
We'd like to think—and the woods and swamp are less
Dangerous than a city street. What sap—

What old-fashioned idiot—would now guide
His guests to the freeway, bus stop, or train?
Some of us men walk our female guests
To the bus stop because we fear her rape,

But is that chivalry? Or a show of might?
And does she feel gratitude or pain?
I stand on my front porch and wave goodbye
To my friends, who run through Seattle rain

To their cars—those covered wagons—and drive
Home alone. Oh, I know my guests will survive—
Please, God, keep them alive—but isn't it sad
That all I've given them is a Google map

That left-rights them out of my neighborhood?
This is a complaint in a minor key
But I hope my guests have always understood
How paranoid I am about their safety.

So, my dear friends, when I ask you to phone
And confirm your arrival home, I hope
You know I'm singing you this love poem,
Grateful that you did find the known road.

On the Second Anniversary of My Father's Death

A bird

(Too big to be a robin,
But still shaped like a robin,
So it might be a robin)

Alights on our deck
And smashes its head
Against the clear glass.

What kind of dumb-ass
Bird thinks it can pass
Through glass like a door?

Amused, I keep score:
Bird 0, Glass 4.
Concussed, that bird learns

A lesson from hurt
And leaves, but returns
The next day to smash

Against the same glass.
How long can this last?
How about six days,

Until that bird's pain
Transforms into rage,
Till bird's rage becomes

Closer to human's,
Then becomes human.
Maddest bird, my wife

Thinks that your crazed flight
Is meant to remind
Me of my father's death,

but I am a poet who distrusts metaphors like a soldier distrusts an unloaded gun. Though I try to forget about the bird, it flies with me (metaphorically speaking) on a business trip, and keeps me awake with its strange songs and stranger needs. Sleepless, I phone home to ask about the bird.

"It was gone for two days," my wife says. "But then it came back and started smashing against the window again. And this time, it brought along a little friend."

"What little friend?" I ask.

"A tiny bird, a sparrow, I think."

"Are they both smashing the glass?"

"No, the little one just watches and sort of cheers on the big one."

"Come on."

"No, really, the little one squawks and tweets and flaps its wings, and I swear, it sounds like it's laughing. Like flying into a window is the funniest thing in the world."

"Well, it is funny. But I don't think the birds realize it's funny."

"I know, I know, but it's funny in a not-funny way, too. I don't know why, but for some reason, I had this thought, so I called that huge bird by your father's name, and guess what happened?"

"Absolutely nothing."

"Well, yeah, almost nothing. But I swear that bird hesitated for a second, and looked at me from the other side of the glass. No, he *regarded* me, and, I know it's crazy to say this, but I think that bird might be your father."

"I think you've been smashing your head against the glass."

"Yeah, maybe. But you know what else? I think that little bird is, like, one of your dad's old, dead drinking buddies, you know? And I'm worried your dad is going to bring home a big flock of his drinking buddies, his birds, and they're going to shit all over the house."

Bird!
Bird!
You are too bird to be my father, too bird,
But you are drunk like my father,

So you could be my father.

Bird, are you my father?

Bird, you might be my father.

Bird, you must be my father.

Bird, you are my father.

Father, you are home.

Father, you are home,

but I lose my faith in transformation two days later as my wife and I sit on our deck and drink coffee.

"Look," she says. "There's your father."

We watch that bird smash its head against our neighbor's upstairs window. Then it flies down to smash against her kitchen window.

I later learn that bird has smashed its head against the windows of the house across the street, and two more houses down the block, and the huge windows of the coffee shop at 34th and Union.

If that bird is my father, then it is also father to every other child in this neighborhood.

After I tell her the story of the bird, a friend writes, "For whatever it's worth, I read once that birds often dive-bomb glass doors because they see another bird in the glass and they think they're attacking that bird, not realizing it's their own reflection—oddly, I think, the way babies are (in an opposite way) amused when they see themselves, as they seem to think it's another child in the mirror, or so I've been told."

Do I see my father in that bird because I see myself in that bird? In my grief and rage, have I grown wings and the need to destroy my own reflection? Do I want to destroy my face because it looks so much like my father's face? I don't want to be that cruel; I don't want to be that hateful. I want to be the child so in love with his father that he falls in love with the parts of his face that most resemble his father's.

I want to pray, but I don't believe in prayer, not today, so I ask my wife, "Why did that bird come to me? What is the meaning of that bird?"

And she says that God delivered unto us this bird to remind us that life is finite and absurd.

Size Matters

1. San Francisco, 1993 & 2003

The journalist and I ate lunch at a waterfront dive—
On a splintered table beneath a tattered umbrella—
Where the crows, one-legged pigeons, and one-eyed gulls survived
By eating French fries, but I still felt like Cinderella

When a sparrow alit on my fist and took a small bite
Out of my sandwich, then another, and another before
It flew away. "These damn birds do that to me all the time,"
I said and sighed, the unspoken bullshit being, of course,

That animals love Indians more than they love white folks.
Self-impressed, I paid for lunch, then a family arrived
And a Down Syndrome woman sat by me and nearly choked
Me with her passionate hug. "Oh, Lila loves the big guys,"

Said her mother as she tried to pull her daughter away,
but I said, "No, it's okay," as I hugged sweet Lila back.
I could see that the journalist was overtly amazed
By my charisma, and though her subsequent review lacked

Reverence, I forgave her, because I knew she'd remember
The day I charmed the birds. But then, ten years later, we met
Again for another interview. We sat together
For lunch one more time, and I said, "I will never forget

"Our first lunch with that woman with Down's and that friendly bird,
The one who ate from my hand." The journalist's poker face
Gave her away. She didn't remember. And, damn, it hurt
To be a big man and yet be so easily erased.

2. Wellpinit, Washington, 2008

On the phone, my mother says, "My neck bones are compressing.
I'm shrinking from arthritis and age and nine pounds of head.
There's nothing I can do. And, son, that's really depressing
Because I'm only going to be three feet tall when I'm dead."

3. Seattle, Washington, 2005

During a field trip, one of my son's small and smart friends
Poked my thick belly and asked, "What are you hiding in there?"
I laughed, but I felt fat, especially in the presence
Of three thin and lovely mothers with perfect skin and hair.

Embarrassed, I imagined that the beautiful mothers
Were all unhappy: one was a drunk; one was bulimic;
And the other was having an affair with her brother-
In-law. None of it was true; I was being sadistic,

So I silently apologized for my cruelty—
For the smallness of my heart. What is the deadly reflex
That requires us to strike at our perceived enemies?
Revenge seems to be as basic as food, shelter, and sex.

But it was Confucius who said, "Before you embark on a journey
Of revenge, dig two graves." I have spent my life in the dirt.
I own a well-worn shovel. My hands are big and bloody,
And I've used them to dig graves and write poems—to hurt and be hurt.

4. Disneyland, California, 1973

One had to be a certain height to ride the Matterhorn
Roller Coaster. As we waited in line, I prayed and hoped
(secretly, of course) that I'd be a few inches too short.
I didn't want to admit that I was scared to the bone

Because I knew that my big brother Arnold and best friend Steve
Would give me shit forever. But I'd had a recent growth spurt,
So I was just tall enough. Forced to grit my balls and teeth,
I climbed into the coaster car. "Who's going to vomit first?"

My brother asked as the chain dragged our car to the summit,
Where we paused for an endless moment before the plummet.
My poor reservation family had won the free jaunt
To Disneyland at an all-you-can-eat restaurant

In Spokane. Photographed, feted, and stunned by our luck,
We made it all the way to Disneyland before the company
That gave us the trip went out of business. Oh, we were fucked.
The restaurant had promised to wire us the money

That would pay for the trip back home. And, yes, we could have skipped
Our day in Disneyland and used that cash to make it back
To the reservation, but that would have been an epic gyp,
So my mother and father, holy fools, spent our small stack

Of money on various amusements. We did make it home
With the charity of Catholic priests and friendly strangers,
But even now, all these years later, it scares me to the bone
To realize that my parents were in love with danger.

5. Plummer, Idaho, 1991

At the six-feet-and-under, all-Indian basketball
Tournament, the big man, Bill Gives, pretended to be short.
He bent his knees and slumped his back until he was six feet tall,
And he remained that height until the first quarter horn

When he unbent and unslumped like a contortionist—
Like a profane yogi—and was suddenly six-foot-five.
There is nobody alive who knows how Bill Gives could twist
Like that, but damn, that Assiniboine owned a magic spine.

6. Portland, Oregon, 2008

In the hotel lobby, Diane saw him first, the fat man
Playing piano while being filmed. She asked, "Who is that?"
I looked over, laughed, and said, "Oh, damn, that's Ron Jeremy,
The porn star." Diane was shocked. "But he's ugly and hairy,"

She said. "Well," I said, "they call him the Hedgehog and his cock
Is twelve inches long. And he has a reality show
On VH1." Diane said, "Well, he can play the piano
Pretty well." I said, "Yeah, I guess he's a smart guy. He taught

Special education before the porn thing. People are
Always surprising." We checked out of the hotel and drove
Away, but then our smallest son asked, "Was that a movie star
In the hotel?" "Kind of," I said, "he has a TV show.

Why do you ask?" My son said, "Because I think I got my face
On camera because the movie star guy smiled at me."
Diane and I looked at each other and then laughed like crazed
Hyenas. Who'd ever guess this would be our reality?

So Diane sent out an email to all of our family
And friends, and said, "If any of you happen to enjoy
Porn stars, then you might already know that Ron Jeremy
has a TV show, and if you watch it, you might see our boy

watching Mr. Jeremy playing a grand piano
in a Portland hotel lobby." None of our friends confessed
to their porn habits or aversions, so I don't know
How many of them prefer their movie stars damp and undressed,

But since porn has grown into a ten billion dollar business—
bigger than the NFL, NBA, and pro baseball
combined—and is now available in forty percent
of U.S. hotel rooms on pay-per-view, I'd guess that all

Of my friends must partake, especially the Willie Lomans—
The sad-ass traveling salesmen and saleswomen—
Who stand at their hotel windows in their best suit or dress
And tremble at the epic scale of their loneliness.

7. Wellpinit, Washington, 1980

In her youth, my grandmother Etta was over six feet tall,
So when she had babies, she quickly earned the name Big Mom,
And though she shrank a bit over time, she was never small.
She was an epic hero, and our tribe depended upon

Her magic. After she was diagnosed with lung cancer,
Tens of thousands of Indians came to say their goodbyes.
She was photographed with chiefs, professors, fancydancers,
poets, drummers, lawyers, priests, and newspaper guys.

My mother keeps those photo albums lined up high on a shelf
In our living room. There's over six feet of organized grief,
And though I know the photos wouldn't interest any thief,
They are my mother's old money—her most substantial wealth.

8. Kamiah, Idaho, 1960

This is my father's story, so who knows if it's the truth,
But he often talked of a ballplayer, a kid named Lee,
A farm boy and high school giant who was the star recruit
At the University of Idaho. Just one week

Before he left for school, Lee swerved to avoid a huge wreck—
A logging truck had knocked over power poles and started a fire.
Lee nearly lost control before he could stop. Then he stepped
Out of his car and brushed his head against a hot wire—

Was electrocuted—and fell instantly dead into the ditch.
My dad said, "If that guy had been only six-foot-seven

120

Or shorter, he would have slipped beneath that wire. It's a bitch,
But poor Lee had to duck his head when he walked into Heaven."

9. Seattle, Washington, 2000 & 2004

When each of our sons turned three, when he could stand on his own,
We stood him against a kitchen wall and measured his growth.
Year by year, he grows up and away—his voice deepens—
And moves closer to that sad and thrilling day when he leaves us.

10. Seattle, Washington, 2008

In *Road House*, one of the worst and, therefore, one of the best
Movies ever made, Patrick Swayze plays a bar bouncer.
But since Swayze is a small guy, he has to puff his chest
And slyly smile whenever any drunk dickpounder

Sidles up to his character, Dalton, and says, "I thought
You'd be bigger." That line is repeated five or six times
During the flick. It's a funny, self-conscious wink and nod
To the audience. There's no way a man of Swayze's size

Could be a bouncer, but wait, I think of Uriah Faber,
An extreme cage fighter who is only five-foot-six
And weighs one hundred and forty-five pounds. But he's laser-
Quick and freakishly strong. I'm much bigger, but he'd kick

My ass in seconds. I'm sure Faber has beaten the hell
Out of plenty of big guys who underestimated
His power. I grew up fighting, but you can't really tell
It by my job description. I suppose I am fated

To always be seen as the poet, effete, shy, and weak,
And I'd love to say that doesn't bother me in the least,
But I would be lying. I am eager to prove my strength,
To metaphorically drop my pants and show you my length,

And yes, that makes me as silly and sad as any guy.
But we can't help ourselves. All of us want to be taller
Than we actually are. All of us lie about our height.
Six feet is the magic number. If a man is smaller

Than that, he'll still insist that he is five-feet-eleven,
Even if he's only five-feet-eight or five-seven.
My father, who was maybe five-ten when he was twenty,
Hated the fact that he'd shrunk to five-six. And he'd baldly

Lie about his height to his doctors and nurses. They knew
He was lying, but he was dying, so maybe the truth
Is more flexible when it comes to death, or maybe it's odd.
Maybe all of us are the same height when we meet our God.

Part 4

Ten Thousand Fathers

Unauthorized

*"When you're running down the street—on fire—people
get the fuck out of your way."*
    —Richard Pryor

I was once hired
To write a biography
Of Richard Pryor.
Proud and inspired,

I wanted to write
The story of Pryor's jokes,
And let his punch lines
Take on independent lives

And identities,
And make them the subjective
Object of study,
Or autobiography.

Yes, I'd planned to make
Pryor's jokes narrate the book.
I'd give Crack a face
And a buddy named Free Base,

And set them afire.
I mean, wouldn't Pryor's jokes
Form an honest choir?
Every man's a liar,

Except on the stage,
So I memorized his jokes,
The externalized rage,
Put ink on the page,

And wrote four chapters,
Then gave a few interviews.
"I am not going after
The easy laughter,"

I said. "I just hope
That I can honor Pryor
By letting his jokes
Come to life and be holy

And wholly real."
But then Pryor's estate called:
"We aren't letting you steal;
Richard's not your meal-

Ticket to glory.
And he never told one joke.
He told stories."
I was suddenly worried

About getting sued,
So I just let the book fade.
During my worst moods,
I wish I had continued,

But I don't blame the Pryors.
After all, it's their story.
They were surrounded by fire
And some of them survived it.

Those last two poetic lines were, of course, the last prose sentence of the biography I was going to write about Richard Pryor. When writing big books, I always write the last sentence first. I need the guidepost, the last stop for my GPS. In my career, I've only kept one pre-written last line all the way to publication, but I think, even though I was hundreds of pages and many months away from publishing Pryor's biography, I might have kept those original last lines, or some variation of them. I know the book needed to begin and end with fire. In fact, in not beginning this poem with fire, I think I made a mistake, so I'm going to go with a new beginning:

Fire was once hired
To write the biography
Of Richard Pryor.
"I am proud and inspired,"

Said Fire. "Mister
Pryor and I go way back.
We had a twisted
Love-hate thing. I wish

We'd got along better.
But, come on, great comedy
Comes from bad weather.
Funny is never tender.

And I've got some guilt
For setting Richard aflame.
But it gives me a thrill
Too, 'cause that joke kills,

The one where you light
A match, and move it
From left to right
(It works best at night),

And say, 'What is this?
It's Richard Pryor running.'
That is some cruel shit
But let me tell you this:

There ain't nothing bad
About laughing at death.
I might have burned the man
But he burned me right back."

And so, now, in resurrecting my prose biography as an obscure poem, I wonder if I'm exploiting Richard Pryor for monetary gain. No way. The devil has never offered to buy a poet's soul. Even Dante, after writing Lucifer's tell-all in terza rima, strolled freely out of the fiery pit. So, even though I write with a ragged and rugged formalism, I think I'm safe. And I don't want to upset the Pryor family. I know other comedians, actors, writers, directors, political activists, and even a few other poets have lauded Richard Pryor. But, damn, has he ever been so publicly celebrated by a reservation-raised Indian? Do you think the Pryors know that Richard's stories gave me courage and hope? (And yes, I agree, I agree, they are stories, not jokes!) After listening to Pryor, after memorizing him, I knew that I could say anything, challenge any convention, and bust any norm. Emily Post was a motherfucker! But, wait, inside Richard Pryor's biography,

I had also wanted to celebrate
The caesura, which is a natural break

Or pause within a line of verse, dictated
By rhythm or sense. I've just created

Three clumsy caesurae in four lines,
But "To err is human; to forgive divine."

Yep, I just quoted Alexander Pope's
Most famous line of verse. Of course, I hope

You held Pope's pause, which stretches across
The vast distance between mortals and God,

And is also completely un-ironic.
So let me turn to someone most comic:

Mr. Henny Youngman, who famously
Asked his audience to "Take my wife, please."

Now, if you rush that joke you'll kill the joke,
So please, take the pause, just like Mr. Pope,

And you will discover that "Take my wife,
Please," uses a caesura with some bite.

So what's the point of this pretentious talk?
Well, poets and comics share a toolbox,

And their geniuses build the same fires,
So when you sing Shakespeare, I sing Pryor.

When Asked What I Think About Indian Reservations, I Remember a Deer Story

Children, have you ever heard a deer scream
After its back legs and spine have been crushed
Beneath the wheels of a logging truck?
That scream is the sound of our grief

After our failed fathers have been crushed.
In Heaven, our dads are still drunk and broke.
Children, you must laugh at the sound of grief,
And at deer bleeding to death on the road,

And at Heaven and fathers all drunk and broke,
Or you will become that deer, torn in half,
Screaming and bleeding to death on the road.
Children, you must escape your bloody past,

Or you will become that deer, torn in half
By the engine it did not understand.
Children, you must escape your bloody past.
Your dead daddy is a dangerous man.

He is the engine you can't understand.
He will steal your food, heat, water, and air.
Your dead daddy is a dangerous man
Who wants all of your grief, but not your prayers.

Grief is your dad's food, heat, water, and air,
And he will feast for years and never quit,
And will demand more grief, but never prayers,
Because he thinks "Prayers don't guarantee shit."

Faithless, he will feast for years and never quit.
He's like the wheels of a logging truck,
Cruel, crushing, and covered with blood and shit.
And you, lonely children, are deer and crushed,

So scream and bleed your way along the road,
Until your lungs, heart, and veins are empty
Of grief, and deny your father's ghost
His last chance to be your warrior-thief.

Independence Day

In a rush, we used an assigned parking space,
And upon our return, the displaced stranger
Said, "That's my spot, you jerk." His rage
Surprised me, but I didn't sense any danger

Until he took five steps toward us. My wife
And sons were suddenly targets, so I knew
I had to protect them. Maybe he had a knife
Or gun. Maybe he was crazy. But his mood

Changed when I stepped out of the shadows.
I'm a big guy, all shoulders and gut and thighs,
And I was not afraid. I grew up trading blows
With bullies, and the man quickly realized

That I would fight hard. Chastened, he retreated
Back toward his car, and with a softer tone,
Said, "Next time, you better leave me a note."
My anger bloomed as my fear receded,

So I stepped fast toward him, and reveled
In his sudden meekness. "Just leave it alone,"
I said, possessed by some childhood devil
Who wanted me to snap and burn the man's bones.

"Stop it," my wife said. "Just get in the car."
She and my sons hurried into their seats,
But I thought I would be admitting defeat
If I did the same. I wouldn't let down my guard

For a moment. I would kill this stranger
And eat his lungs, stomach, heart, thumbs, and eyes.
I became the one in love with danger.
Ashamed, I shouted, "Have a safe Fourth of July!"

And looked at the man for the first time.
He was rude, Napoleonic, and weak.
Just back from work, he didn't want to fight.
He wanted to sit on his couch and watch TV.

The man gave me the finger, but I just waved
And climbed into our car. Contrite and dazed,
I mumbled an apology to my wife,
"I thought the man was threatening our lives."

"I know," she said. "You had to back him off.
And you did that. You proved you were tough.
But then you got mean." And yes, it was shitty.
I took the man's space and his dignity.

Is it surprising that I know how to be cruel?
My entire career is based on revenge.
I think of my sons, so tender and new,
And how they'd witnessed me walk to the edge

And nearly begin the long, harrowing drop
Before I heeded their mother's call to stop.
I know my boys had so many questions
But I failed to give them this lesson:

Sons, what I did to that man was wrong;
There can be that much weakness in being strong.

Cryptozoology

I saw a crow, with a row of blue feathers
Persisting down its back, perched on the wall
Squaring our front yard. I wanted to call
To my wife, but knew that silence was better

because my voice—any voice—would have scared
The bird into escape. I have seen crows with gray
Or white feathers, but never with feathers jay-
Blue and luminous. "Was this mutation rare?"

I wondered. "Or maybe this is not a crow."
But no, that bird had the head, eyes, and beak
Of a crow. I'm not a birder, but I've seen
Enough crows to identify one. I know

You think I'm telling yet another story—
My friend, the amateur ornithologist
And full-time cynic, thinks I'm full of shit—
But I swear that I witnessed this odd glory

Of a crow that is the only one of its kind—
A bird that is the only member of its tribe.

Missed Connections

at the Santa Barbara Airport

Descending, in our forty-seat airplane,
I saw an older man had parked his car
At the edge of the runway. He waved
At us, so I waved, but we were too far

Apart to see each other, and he was not
Welcoming me anyway. Near the back
Of the plane, a woman, hair in a knot,
Clutching a tattered Vintage paperback,

Waved and smiled and hugged her seatmate.
"That's my husband," she said. "I haven't seen
Him in ten years. It's so great, it's so great."
She shook and wept; it was quite a scene—

A mystery—and I was hungry to know
Why a wife and husband had lived apart
For a decade. I wanted to ask, but no,
I decided to imagine the parts

They'd been playing: She was the Red Cross
Nurse who'd been kidnapped by militant
Rebels, then blindfolded and marched across
The border, but he'd remained diligent

For ten epic years, pressuring despots
And presidents, until the March dawn
When Australian tourists spotted
Her staggering across a Thai hotel lawn.

Starved and weak, she fell into their arms.
"I've been released," she said. "I've been released."
Traded for ammunition and small arms,
And treated for malnutrition and disease,

She was only now, six weeks after rescue,
Reuniting with her husband. She was first
Off the airplane—we all gave her the room—
And she, aching with a different thirst,

Burst through the security gates
And rushed into her husband's embrace.
Later, after they had gone, as I waited
For my bags, I saw a friendly face—

A young woman who'd just witnessed
What I'd witnessed. I wiped away tears.
"Ten years," I said. "I'd die from the stress."
"Oh, no," she said. "It wasn't ten years.

It was ten days." Jesus, I had misheard
The old woman and created glory
Out of the ordinary. Just one word,
Misplaced, turned a true and brief story

Into a myth. And, yes, it was lovely
To see how the long-in-love can stay
In love. But who truly gets that lonely
After only ten days away?

I thought I had witnessed an epic—
A Santa Barbara elderly Odyssey—
But it was something more simplistic.
It was a love story, small and silly,

And this is cruel, but here's my confession:
Depending on the weather or my mood,
I'll repeat the myth because it's more impressive
Than something as clear and bright as the truth.

March Madness

"*UCLA 73, GONZAGA 71*"
—NCAA Basketball Tournament, 2006

*"All the interests of my reason,
speculative as well as practical,
combine in the three following questions:*
    1. What can I know?
    2. What ought I to do?
    3. What may I hope?"
—Immanuel Kant

*"I can't believe it. I just watched
that replay like he was going to make
the shot this time."*
—Randall Olsen

When Batista missed the shot, I wanted
To punch God. Lord, why did you steal the game
From these young men, these Bulldogs, now haunted

By reasonable ghosts who paraphrase Kant
(*Why did you hope?*) as they rattle their chains?
When Batista missed the shot, I wanted

To know what I ought to do for the gaunt
Adam Morrison who, despite his fame,
Is only a young man; He will be haunted

Forever by this loss. Taunting and taunted,
Morrison collapsed to the floor in sorrowful rage
When Batista missed the shot. I wanted

To know what I could know, but felt daunted
By a godless God. Lord, can you explain
Why you've pushed these young men down the haunted

Descent into the hell of self? Vaunted
God, absurd God, why must they prove their faith?
When Batista missed the shot, I wanted

Him to shoot again. I wanted him to flout
Space and time, make the hoop, and win the game
For these young men, these Bulldogs. I'm haunted

By missed shots and missing fathers. I lost
My dad to vodka, but I kept his name.
I miss him most in March. I always want
To call him and talk about the big games,

About the Shakespearean comedy
And tragedy of the NCAA.
We talked hoops because it was easy
To show emotion; it was the only way

To show emotion. If he were alive,
He'd say, "The world is filled with white boys
Who know how to lose and how to survive,
But we Injun boys just make rhythmic noise."

My father, my drum, you were the all-star
Of hopeless and blood and orphan and scar.

My father, my drum, you were the all-star
Of hook shot and broken tooth and wrecked cars.

My father, my drum, you were the all-star
Of hesitate and lost and shooting guard.

My father, my drum, you were the all-star
Of the halfway tattoo, the unstarted start.

My father, my drum, you were the all-star
Of man-to-man D and congestive heart.

My father, my drum, you were the all-star
Of screen and zone and lonesome and hot arm.

My father, my drum, you were the all-star
Of hover and quit and freeze and stop.

Reading Light

Startled awake,
I curse. I hate

The hours I've lost
To turn and toss,

The grind of mind
And teeth. This night,

Like each night
Of my weary life,

I shamble down-
Stairs and look around

The kitchen for junk
To eat and eat. Fuck!

I am old and fat! And I cannot sleep! I wish there were a cure for insomnia. But there's not. No, all one can do is eat and read and eat and read. W.C. Fields said, "The best cure for insomnia is to get lots of sleep." Lydia Davis said, "Insomnia is the wish for immortality granted by an ass." Plato said, "Insomnia is the genocide of the soul." Wait, I'm lying. Plato didn't say that. Plato had nothing to say about insomnia. What do I have to say about insomnia? Well, let me tell you about the saddest music in the world:

When you hear the birds sing
To greet the pre-dawn light

And you have not slept well
Or not at all that night—

As you have not slept well
On one thousand such nights—

You learn that being awake
Can feel like being at a wake.

Abraham Lincoln said, "An insomniac is a house divided against itself and cannot
stand." Oscar Wilde said, "An insomniac cannot be too careful in his choice
of enemies." Jane Austen wrote, "An insomniac's imagination is very rapid; it
jumps from admiration to love, from love to matrimony in a moment." Emily
Dickinson wrote, "Because I could not stop for sleep / Sleeplessness stopped for
me." Hamlet said, "To sleep or not to sleep: that is the question." But wait, as I
eat and read and eat and read, I hear a noise upstairs. What is it?

Laughter? Joy?
My older boy

Lies awake.
"It's late," I say.

"You need to sleep."
"I need to read,"

He says. "This book
Is really good.

It makes me laugh.
Dad, please, I have

Five more pages."
Oh, at his age,

I read like this.
So I hug and kiss

My son goodnight.
"Turn out the light,"

I say, "when you finish, you little rebel." Laughing, I walk back downstairs to eat and read some more. How could I punish my son for reading, no matter that he'd have to drag his tired ass to school in the morning and would likely fall asleep sitting at his desk sometime in the mid-afternoon? It reminds me of Damon Wayans, who said that it was impossible for a standup comedian like him to discipline his kids for being smart asses. "All I can really do," Wayans said, "is tell them they need to work on their timing." I suppose I could discipline my bookworm son by making him read more challenging novels, but what kind of brutal father dictates his children's reading lists? I want my boys to read everything! There's a rule in my house that my sons can buy any book anytime they want. The book-buying budget is unlimited! Oh, God, I wish I'd grown up in a house like the one my wife and I are creating. Oh, God, let me be happy and insomniac for a few minutes. And so I am, so I am. And after I've eaten a bag of tortilla chips and read twenty pages of murder mystery, I go to check on my older son and find that he's asleep with his book on his chest. My younger son is also asleep with a book on his chest.

Lord, I am awake at three,
And I'm half-depressed and half-manic,

But my sons sleep easily.
My prayers might be pitiful and frenetic,

But I still thank God
That my insomnia is not genetic.

Ten Thousand Fathers

Everywhere fathers are dying or dead,
The wells are empty of water, and we
Cannot tell the difference between drought
And grief, or between fathers and water,

Because we are seventy-eight percent
Water before we die and seventy-
Eight percent father after the last shouts
Of crash teams who've saved ten thousand fathers

But could not save the only one. All beds
Are deathbeds. Please, children, demand to see
The list of fathers who faded, fell out,
And died in the same bed where your father

Faded and fell. Children, what can be said
To bring fathers back? Nothing, nothing. We
Only conjure ghosts, or parts of ghosts. Count
The disembodied hands that slapped skin, stirred

Coffee, pulled us by braids, dropped us in beds,
Dragged us through amusements, danced us off-key
Across wood and carpet, shoved us past bouts
With bullies and hunger, loved our mothers

Or some other child's mother. Wedded
To our fathers, alive or dead, can we
Ever divorce, separate, leave, run out,
Abandon or exorcise? As water

Always returns to water, so all dead
Fathers return to their children, as we,
Always small and childish in our doubts,
Curse and praise and curse and praise our fathers.

Thrash

1.

In the Park Place Hotel, I need to piss
(It is so lovely to piss near the rich),
So I make my way to the lobby head
(O, porcelain, O, brass) and unzip next

To an elder gent in a bespoke suit.
He stares down at my penis, which is cute
And sienna, so this old white man must
Love the barely exotic. I am touched

By his frank lust as he watches me splash.
I wonder if he's going to make a pass,
But then he whispers, "Kid, you should thank God
That you're young. I've been here squeezing out drops

For five minutes." We laugh at his candor
(How glorious his lack of staid manners),
But I wonder if he laughs about death
When he climbs, nude and wrinkled, into bed

With the lovely woman who remembers
A young man who was more hard than tender.

2.

Oh, damn, can you believe I claimed

To own a cute penis? Does fame,
However pathetic, force guys

To fall in love with their rhymes
As they fall in love with their cocks?

144

Long ago, in college, I walked
Out of a poetry reading

Because the famous man needed
To read an argyle and tweed

Ode to his vasectomy.
"Who cares? Who cares? Who the fuck cares?"

I asked as I climbed the backstairs
And complained my way to the bar.

What kind of cold and dying star
Could write such a narcissistic,

Matter-sucking poem about his dick?
Well, twenty years later, I shaved

My pubic hair, then, raw and razed,
Reclined in the doctor's cold room

As he tugged my sperm-transport tubes
Out of a slice in my scrotum,

Held both between a finger and thumb,
Cut each into halves, then sealed

The ends and tucked the whole deal
Back inside. Briefly, I felt sad

For the children I wouldn't have,
But the doctor looked at my face

And asked, "Aren't you the one who made
The movie about that liar?

"What was his name? Builds-the-Fire?"
Trisected, I cursed my small fame

And its huge friends, ego and shame,
Then went home to ice my empty

Balls with a bag of frozen peas.

3.

As I helped my young son pee
In a public restroom, he

Gazed lovingly up at me
And shouted, "Daddy! Daddy!

Someday my penis is going to be bigger than your penis!"

That's my boy, my progeny,
Who owes half his genes to me,

And who turned a truck stop Denny's
Into a Greek tragedy.

4.

My friend watched his baby's circumcision,

Saw the blood and heard the terrible cries,
And, distraught, wondered why that tradition

Continues. "But the worst thing is that I
Never questioned it," he said. "They cut me,

So I cut my son." Dear friend, I wonder
If we practice other forms of butchery,

If we worship the knife, if we blunder
Our way into blade and bandage and blood

Only because our fathers never thought
To ask why a peaceful and loving God

Wants us to sacrifice parts of our cocks?
"I won't do this to another baby,"

My friend said. "And I will apologize
To my son for this blood ceremony,

And hope that he someday forgives, or tries
To forgive me." Dear friend, forgive my lack

Of tact, but did you know the doc severed
Thousands of nerves that will never grow back?

These cock-stigmata will not get better,
And though some think that I exaggerate

The size of the wounds, I quietly mourn
My loss of sense, of what I cannot replace,

Of what was stolen when I was newborn.

5.

On an episode of *ER*, when a mother and father are contemplating circumcision, Maria Bello, playing a resident, says, "Frankly, I find circumcised penises to be more aesthetically pleasing."

Although Ms. Bello was acting and not necessarily advocating her personal opinion of circumcision, I still found the scene to be strangely erotic. I am often surprised by what I find erotic. Is your libido as unpredictable as mine? Do you find Maria Bello to be a sexy person? How do you feel about penises?

Years later, while watching *The Cooler*, I was happy to discover that Maria Bello had shot a completely nude love scene with William H. Macy. And while Ms. Bello is certainly gorgeous, I was most aroused by the cellulite on the backs of her thighs. Those capsules of fat made her feel more like a fragile and finite person than a manufactured actor. And though we do get to see Mr. Macy's flat and pale ass, we don't get to find out whether he's circumcised or not.

"Um, Maria, how you doing? These love scenes make me really uncomfortable."

"Yeah, Bill, but let's use it, okay? I mean, if we were going to make love for the first time in the real world, we'd feel this nervous, too."

"Yeah, yeah, I know. But this is the first time anybody has ever asked me to show my ass. It's not a movie star ass."

"Hey, it's not like I have Nicole Kidman's ass."

"Oh, you're beautiful, Maria. And your ass should be bronzed."

"Thank you, Bill. That's very kind of you."

"You're welcome. And, um, I hate to be so forward, but, the thing is, if I get an erection during the love scene, I hope you won't be offended."

"I'll be flattered, Bill."

"Oh, that's great. Well, it's good, I guess. And I hope you won't be offended if I don't get an erection."

"Well, I won't be offended, but my character might be."

"That's funny."

"Yeah, and speaking of funny, can I ask you a personal question?"

"Sure."

"Are you circumcised?"

6.

And now I pause to confess
That some have taken offense
At my public willingness
To rant and rave about sex,

To be less than serious
About the meaning of lust.
Some think I've betrayed their trust,
That I've said far too much

About blowjobs, shit, and piss.
They might be right about this.

This poem might be free of wit.
It might be callow and sick,

But if I can't praise and curse
The size and shape of our thirsts,

Using any of the words,
Profane or not, that I've learned,

Then why should I write or speak?
I think some readers want me

And my vocabulary
To conform, comfort, and please.

They don't want to watch me thrash
Through blood, bile, cum, and trash.

They don't want to hear me laugh
At sex, pussy, cock, and ass.

They think that a funny poem
Is not a serious poem.

They think that a dirty joke
Is only a dirty joke.

But don't those fools realize
That I am always surprised

By the beauty of this life?
Don't they ever laugh and cry

at the gorgeous absurdities of sex? Like the time back in college, when my
girlfriend and I heard the pitiful and pained wail of a cat in the night, and we went
out with flashlight and food to investigate, and found an older female cat pressed
tightly to the sidewalk while a dumb young male tom clumsily tried to fuck her.

"Oh, look," my girlfriend said. "She's really pissed that he doesn't know
how to do it. Jeez, all he's doing is frustrating her."

"I hope I'm not that incompetent," I said.

"You used to be. But you're getting better."

"Thank you. I think."

"You know, back when I was first starting to think about sex, I'd see dogs or horses or cats doing it, and I'd get all horny and jealous."

"How does it make you feel now?" I asked.

"It just makes me feel horny," she said.

So my girlfriend and I went back to my apartment and fucked for hours (well, maybe for an hour). And every once in a while, she wailed like an angry cat.

"More! More! More!" she shouted. "Better! Better! Better!"

7.

At twenty-five minutes past the hour
(And already thirty-five minutes late),
I saunter naked out of the shower
And startle the iPodded Slavic maid,

Who steps backward, points at my dampish crotch,
Whispers a quick prayer in her mother tongue,
Then, to save us, makes the sign of the cross.
Corrupted, on fire, she turns and runs

Out of the four-star room. In Catholic shock,
I step in front of the oak full-length mirror
And stare at the folds and curves of my cock,
Which has never caused such mortal fear

In any lover's and/or stranger's eyes.
My Lord, I confess. It's all my fault.
Though my sins are only average-sized,
I turned a faithful woman into salt.

8.

I stand accused of the crime of thrash, which means that I write and talk without understanding why my rage, love, humor, lust, and hate often feel

150

like one minuscule and/or epic emotion. It means that I want the random mix of heat and insincerity in this poem to approximate the random mix of heat and insincerity in my life. I plead guilty as charged.

Oh, Lord, I thrash.
Oh, Lord, I enter into the thrash.
Oh, Lord, I am thrash.

9.
And now I remember to say:
When we celebrate our birthdays,

We celebrate our conception
And honor our parents' passions.

So, thank you, Father and Mother
For fucking and sucking each other.

I celebrate my mother's egg.
I celebrate my father's sperm.

I honor the need to get laid.
I honor my lovely, bloody birth.

10.

My uncle, small-bladdered and diabetic, was reservation-famous because he had to piss every fifteen minutes. But we don't know if his bladder's size was the primary factor in his frequent urination, or if he had weakened his bladder by insisting on stopping and peeing no matter where he was.

"Uncle," I said to him. "You trained your bladder like you house train a puppy. You get a little urge and you're whining and scratching at the front door."
He laughed. No, he slid his dentures into his mouth and laughed. He hated to laugh without his teeth.

Over the years, my uncle peed on every dirt road leading off Highway 2. He peed between and behind buildings in Wellpinit, Springdale, Chewelah, Colville, Cusick, Reardan, Davenport, all over Eastern Washington.

My uncle once peed into a storm drain in the Disneyland parking lot.

When I was six, he stopped his station wagon on Interstate 90, halfway between the Division and Maple Street exits, and emptied his bladder while hundreds of cars rushed past him. My aunt, my cousins, and I laughed and ducked our heads, but my uncle, always a friendly man, waved hello to the good people of Spokane.

Near the end of his life, my uncle used more bedpans than toilets, and felt like a child in doing so. After surgery to remove a benign but gigantic tumor, my uncle, so desperate to prove his strength, crawled out of bed, dragged his IV pole to the bathroom, and emptied his bladder. He didn't quite make it to the toilet, but he figured the floor was an essential part of the bathroom, and was therefore an acceptable target.

Our compensations define our character.

My uncle was good with crosswords and puns, and better with intentional and unintentional malaprops, and loved to read, but he was not a wise man. However, he was street-smart and romantic. Though he only peed while standing, he taught his sons and nephews to pee while sitting down.

"Boys," he said, "you can't expect a woman to love your penis if she has to clean up after it."

11.

When I was thirteen and clumsy,

I dropped a cup of boiling tea
On my crotch. I quickly pulled off

My clothes, but not quickly enough,
As the tea burned me to the first,

Second, and third degree. That hurt
Was epic and original.

On all fours like an animal,
I crawled, naked and new, upstairs

And into the living room, where
My mother, my source of power,

Pushed me into an ice-cold shower
And called for the rez EMTs,

Who inexpertly treated me
As they rushed me to the ER.

Morphined, I was a rock star
Who soloed three choruses of curses

While scores of doctors and nurses
Arrived at my bedside to gawk

At the dumb kid who had burned his cock.

12.

Q: When the poet describes his mother as being his "source of power," what
do you think that means?

    a.   That he must enjoy and endure an Oedipal relationship with her.
        After all, he was a teenage boy running naked into his mother's
        arms.
    b.   That he would have described a dog, or even a cockroach, as being
        his "source of power," if said dog or cockroach had pushed him
        and his blistering crotch into an ice-cold shower. In other words,

the source of power was the ice-cold shower. But you can forgive the poet for his confusion. After all, his balls were on fire.

c.   That power rhymes with shower.

d.   Many aboriginal cultures are matriarchal. The poet and his mother's tribe, the Spokane, are historically matriarchal, if not in current practice. So the poet is paying homage to his mother in a flaccid attempt to bring gender equality into a poem about penises.

e.   Or to put it in more literary terms, the poet, feeling far too assimilated while writing a semi-formal poem that features Western Civilized rhyme, syllabics, and meter, tried to "Indian up" the damn thing by bringing his mother into it.

f.   I don't really care about the power thing. I'm still wondering why the poet thinks he can get away with rhyming "gawk" with "cock."

g.   All of the above.

13.

My lovely sons are uncircumcised.

When I first wrote that sentence, I mistyped "songs" instead of "sons." So I had to circumcise a letter in order to correct my error. Do you think that's a coincidence?

My lovely songs are uncircumcised.

14.

When I was ten, my
Best friend X and I
Stumbled in on Y

Jacking off into
A can of Crisco.
I didn't yet know

How inventive boys
Can be with their toys.
But these feral joys

Easily transform
Into acts of war.
I think of the horrors

of soldiers gang-raping civilian women and children during Sand Creek and the
Vietnam War. I think of the rape camps built in Nanking and Bosnia. Can you
imagine the life of a woman in those camps? Can you imagine the very creation
of a rape camp? Can you imagine being raped dozens of times by dozens of men?
Hundreds of rapes, hundreds of men. Thousands of rapes, thousands of men. I
think of Ted Bundy and Gary Ridgeway, of the dozens of famous and nameless
serial killers who have hunted, are hunting, and will hunt women. I think of
the reservation Indian boy terrorists who put paper bags over their heads and
videotaped their gang rape of an Indian woman. Imagine the life of that Indian
woman, who had to move away from her reservation after she was brutalized.

Q: What kind of God allows this?
A: A male God.

15.

But that which makes men beasts

Also makes us angels.
Do you recall the best

Sex, the tender angles
Of a man's hard body,

His laughter in bed,
His eyes like a boy's

When you let him be
The first to caress

The scars that replaced your breasts?

16.

Whenever I walk into a Barnes & Noble, I feel like Pavlov's dog because I immediately have to go to the bathroom. Don't ask me to explain this reflexive phenomenon. So, last November, in the University Village store, I raced into the bathroom, lucked into an empty stall, pulled down my pants, and sat. But as I sat, I passed gas very loudly. No, that's not exactly right. I exploded. And kept exploding. When the explosions subsided, the guy in the next stall shouted, "Speak to me, O, one-eyed monster!"

17.

Q: How would you describe the general tone of Section 16?
    a.   Repulsive
    b.   Juvenile
    c.   Freudian
    d.   Hilarious
    e.   All of the above

Q: How would you describe the tone of this entire poem?
    a.   Callow
    b.   Phallocentric
    c.   Jungian
    d.   Hilarious
    e.   All of the above

Q: I love the man who shouted, "Speak to me, O, one-eyed monster!" How does that make you feel?
    a.   Curious about its homoerotic undertones.
    b.   Repulsed by its homoerotic overtones.
    c.   Aroused by its homoerotic midtones.
    d.   Amazed by my random and magical interaction with a complete stranger.
    e.   None of the above.

Q: All twelve men in the bathroom, including me, burst into laughter after the guy shouted, "Speak to me, O, one-eyed monster!" What does this signify?

a. That the poet is vainly trying to graft literary meaning onto a poop joke.
b. That all men are assholes.
c. That the image of a talking anus is universal and, therefore, makes this poem a multicultural study of essential body functions.
d. That a good joke is a good joke, no matter where it's told.
e. I don't know.

Q: This entire poem contains overt and covert references to God, Jesus, the Holy Ghost, Christianity, penises, and talking anuses. How does that make you feel?
a. Shocked by the blasphemy.
b. Convinced that the poet is a closeted homosexual.
c. Even more convinced that the poet is a secular terrorist.
d. Thoroughly convinced that the poet is, in fact, a practicing Roman Catholic.
e. Suddenly aware that if God did make humans in God's image, then God must have a penis and an anus, as well as a vagina, and is, in fact, androgynous.
f. Unaware that the poet has made any reference to the Holy Ghost.

18.

In Chicago-O'Hare, I raced,
With full bladder, from the airplane
To the nearest urinal, faced
A wall of adverts that proclaimed,
IN CAPITALS, the epic grace
Of The Windy City, a nickname

That has never once tempted me
To favor the place. So I peed
And thought of cities less windy,
When I happened to glance and see
Two boys, ages seven and three,
And their father, a family

Of full bladders, step up to use
The next urinal. The older knew
How it worked. He unzipped his blue
Jeans and let his little lion loose.
But the younger boy only mewed,
"Daddy, Daddy, what do I do?"

The dad unzipped his younger's jeans
And said, "Little man, you can pee
Beside your brother." So, with glee,
The boys played a tender and sweet
Duet (like my brother and me),
And giggled when they crossed their streams.

19.

Q: In Section 18, when the brothers cross urine streams, what are the
geopolitical repercussions?
    a.   It suggests that if mortal enemies, such as George W. Bush and
         Osama Bin Laden, crossed their streams, then we would all live
         in a much safer world.
    b.   It proves that boys are not naturally homophobic, and will
         happily and proudly display their penises in public, without
         fear of other males' opinions and/or desires.
    c.   It reveals that males develop the need to mark their territory at
         a very young age, and that these particular brothers will likely
         grow up to be Special Forces soldiers, and will fight and maybe
         die in the same war.
    d.   It crassly and poetically illuminates the love that a good father
         can have for his good sons.
    e.   Come on, man, it's just an airport bathroom, okay?

20.

Young men! Old men! Cross your streams
And your souls will be redeemed!

21.

My wife is smarter than me, and has a master's degree in theology, so I often ask her about God.

"Hey, D," I say over the telephone. "Does God have a penis?"

"Jesus has one," she says, "but I don't think God has one."

"So the son has a penis and the father doesn't? That doesn't make sense, does it?"

"It isn't about sense. Your question is sort of beside the point. God isn't corporeal. To give God a penis, to even talk about the possibility of God's penis, or God's vagina for that matter, you have to anthropomorphize God. And you really can't talk about God in those human terms."

"So you're saying that God has moved beyond the penis."

"God probably existed before the penis."

"What about the Holy Ghost? Does the Holy Ghost have a penis?"

"Now you're being silly. Get off the phone. I have to put the kids to bed."

"No, come on, I'm trying to engage you in a serious theological discussion."

"No, you're trying to get me say something funny or strange or original so you can put it in your poem. You've run out of ideas so you're trying to steal ideas from me."

"And you have a problem with that?"

"Right now, I do."

"Just tell me, okay? Does the Holy Ghost have a penis?"

"Well, in many traditions, the Holy Ghost is female. So what do you think?"

"The Holy Ghost probably doesn't need a penis."

"Probably not."

"Okay, okay, just one more question, okay?"

"What?"

"Will we have penises in Heaven?"

"Will we have penises in Heaven? What does that mean? Am I going to have a vagina? Are we going to switch sexual organs? Are we all going to have both? We might not have bodies at all. We might be incorporeal. Think about that. What will it mean to your faith if you wake up in the afterlife with an incorporeal penis? Will we have penises in Heaven? I can only tell you with certainty that I won't."